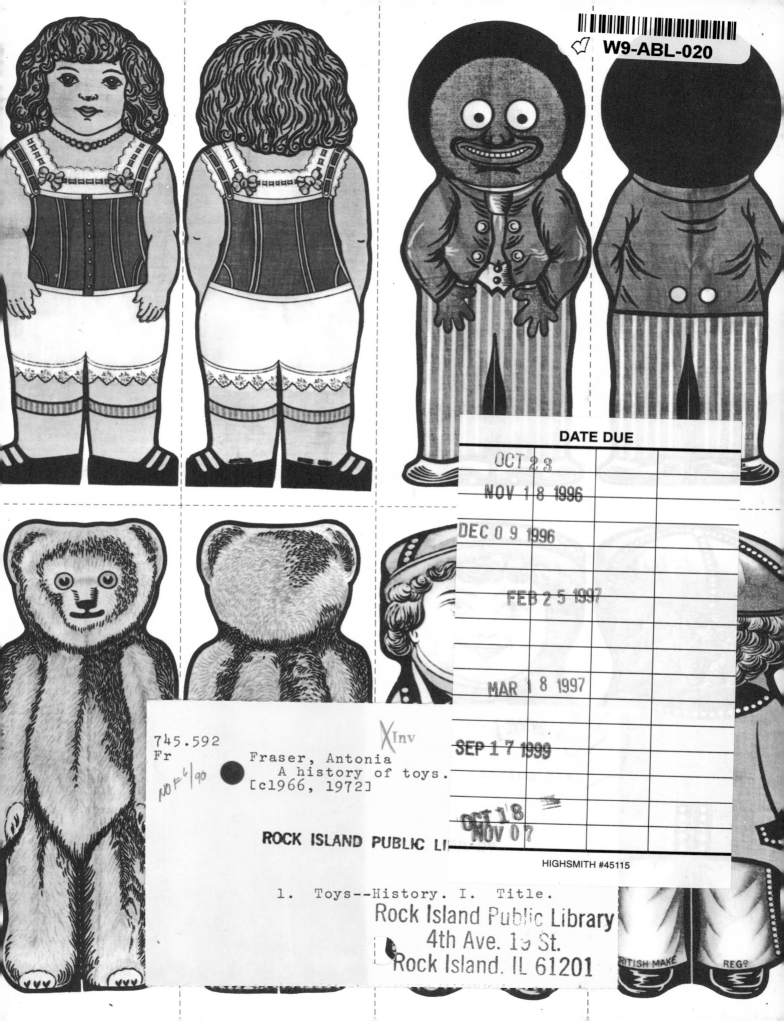

a history of

Antonia Fraser

Spring Books

London · New York · Sydney · Toronto

Original edition published 1966 and ©
copyright 1966 by George Weidenfeld &
Nicolson Ltd, London
Designed by Colin Banks and John Miles

This edition published 1972 by
The Hamlyn Publishing Group Limited
London · New York · Sydney · Toronto
Hamlyn House, Feltham, Middlesex,
England

Printed in Germany by K. G. Lohse,
Graphischer Grossbetrieb
Frankfurt am Main

ISBN 0 600 34387 1

TO
REBECCA, FLORA, BENJAMIN, NATASHA
AND DAMIAN FRASER
who first inspired and then impeded the
writing of this book

Contents

1 The Nature of Toys

1 As long ago as the age of the Ancient Greeks the doll was a companion of an idle hour

The nature of toys is compounded of pleasure, fantasy and imitation. The history of toys is made up of contrasts, and lies somewhere between the needs of the child, the interest of the historian, the desire of the collector, and, last but not least, the involvement of the adult in his childhood – the magic world, from which he cannot bear to be excluded forever by the mere act of growing-up.

But if the nature of toys is to give pleasure, is the subject worthy of a history at all? Or are toys merely charming trifles to be loved, abandoned or destroyed? There are certainly occasions and references galore in history and literature which point to the toy as a mere pretty appendage of life. When Bottom in *A Midsummer Night's Dream* offered to make Titania 'brooches and toys for her delight' there was no suggestion of seriousness in his purpose; he was extending the lightest most frivolous offering in his power. The toy, then, is a delightful object which gives pleasure, a companion of an idle hour, something far removed from the earnestness of existence. But at this point memories of one's own childhood break in. Was the beloved Teddy really only a plush filled object of some psychological significance ... one's mind rebels from the idea. No, indeed, he was the companion of one's dreams.

The French writer, Louise de Vilmorin, tells the story of her doll Lili – 'elle régnait au centre de ma vie d'enfant' – and illustrates the sort of dreadful infant tragedy which can arise when a conflict occurs between the involved passion of the child and the unthinking indifference of the adult. Lili had brown hair, taken from the governess's own head, and clothes copied in miniature from her owner's. She led a pampered life in the nursery, until one day Madame de Vilmorin asked the maid to run upstairs and bring down the nearest toy, as she needed something quickly to give away. In this casual manner, Lili was reft from her absent owner. Despair of the little girl! Worse still, it was too late to recover the beloved object, which its new owner, with unbelievable callousness, had left on a train. Louise de Vilmorin wanted to wear mourning for her lost love, but was forbidden to do so by the cruel denizens of a grown-up world.

Perhaps each childhood conceals somewhere within it a similar tragedy – forgotten but not forgiven. One is reminded of the song of Mrs Doasyouwouldbedoneby in *The Water Babies*, whose 'prettiest doll in the world' was lost on the heath to the terrible detriment of her appearance, paint washed away, arm trodden off by cows, hair uncurled, yet to her owner:

> For old sakes' sake, she is still, dears
> The prettiest doll in the world.

Toys and dolls, these companions of a child's fantasy, can be as old and mended as you please, the sawdust dripping out of their bodies, and yet the fantasy will be just as potent. Many toys in history have indeed been astonishingly transient – in conception as well as fact. We have all seen gingerbread men and animals, and been captivated by them, before firmly eating them. In eighteenth-century Germany some of the most popular toys were made of gum tragacanth, an essentially transient material. Peter III of Russia is even said to have sentenced a rat, who nibbled at one of them, to be court martialled. Paper dolls, whether of the simple child's sort, or of the more elaborate eighteenth-century German variety, surely gain a certain charm from their ephemeral quality. Folk dolls, made of such material as corn husks and palm leaves, are also innately transient, and I often think they look strangely bewildered when preserved in museums for sociological interest, compared to their aristocratic cousins, the antique dolls and automata. Yet their impermanent nature has never robbed them of their aura of fantasy.

A charming example of doll-make-believe is told of the children of Lord Lytton by G.W.E.Russell. The Lytton children were dressing up: 'The scene displayed a Crusader knight returning from the wars. At his gate he was welcomed by his wife, to whom he recounted his triumphs and the number of heathen he had slain. His wife, pointing to a row of dolls of various sizes replied with pride: "And I too my lord, have not been idle".'

It is the importance of make-believe in toys which bridges the gap between the element of fantasy and the element of imitation. With regard to imitation, it is often mechanical toys which enable a child to learn something about his surroundings; he reproduces in a car, train, or boat or aeroplane, the elements of the mechanical world which fascinates him, in Wordsworth's lines:

> As if his whole vocation
> Were endless imitation.

At first children want to push a car or train across the floor themselves – to be the actual impulse of action. Later they become fascinated by the mechanics of movement and demand that every car should have an engine, because real cars have engines. But whether the child pushes the train along the floor (figure 250), or winds it up, or ignites some elaborate steam process, his basic desire is still the same – to imitate the world around him. Pleasure, fantasy and now imitation therefore seem to be the first three elements in the nature of toys.

Of the three, it is fantasy which seems to develop a toy into something more important than a mere trifle. If toys are the starting-point of dreams, then the nature of children's toys must be of extreme importance, not only in forming their fantasies,

2 The instinct for imitation which lies at the root of many toys – a girl with her doll copying a mother with her baby – illustrated in one of a series of stylized engravings published in France in 1820 under the title Le Bon Genre

3 Ever since the early days of the steam engine children have been playing with toy trains. An intricate fretwork model of a North Eastern Railway Class based on plans issued by 'Hobbies' early this century

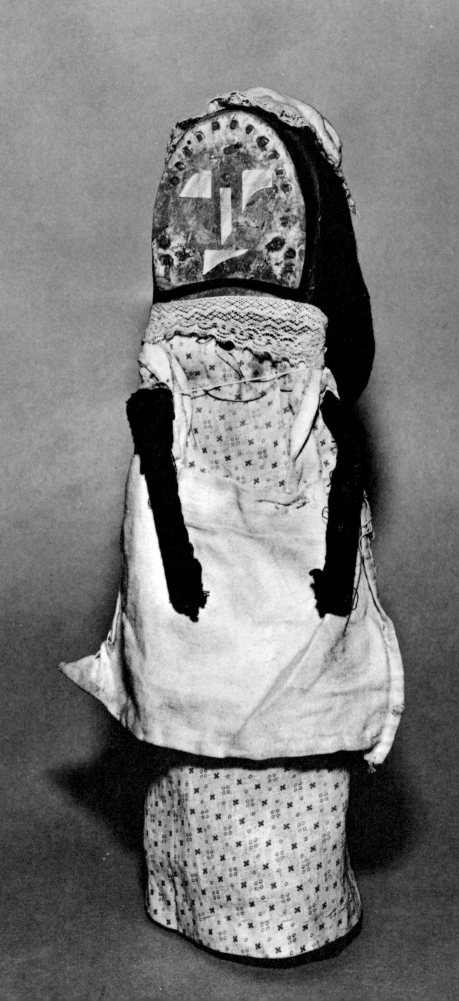

arms and hair; a poor child's doll from
London, dated about 1905. Throughout
history children have adapted the
simplest materials to make emergent
toys*

but also in guiding what sort of fantasies they form. Already the natural frivolity of a toy begins to dissolve and the toy becomes a vital clue to the self-expression of children, and hence later to their adult behaviour.

In a famous book of the 1930s, *Intellectual Growth in Young Children*, Susan Isaacs maintained that since in all their free play children are working out their fears and fantasies, the nature of their toys must be of enormous importance. She believed that toys helped them to accept the limitations of the world, and to control their real behaviour – in short, to pass from a dream world into a real world. Psychoanalysis reveals that profoundly symbolic meanings are attached by children to objects as diverse as engines, motors, fires, lights, animals, water and mud. This is indeed a far cry from the notion of toys as innocent companions of leisure. Who knows, for example, what terrible reactions were set off in the breast of a friend of the author who was given a sword for Christmas, and then beaten with it only a fortnight later? The unfairness of the grown-up world could hardly have been demonstrated more cruelly.

So now we have two completely disparate elements in the nature of toys. On the one hand we have their essential charm – the nostalgia which keeps the worn teddy bear on the bed of the famous poet (figure 5), the ragged doll in the film star's dressing room, and on the other, their deep importance in the psychological development of a child and therefore presumably of the human race throughout its history.

This second aspect of toys leads to the vital distinction between a good toy and a bad toy. In *Play and Toys in Nursery Years* Dr Hart describes three *good* toys: those which stimulate the imagination and invite effort, like building blocks; those which help a child attain adult skill, like scissors and brushes and brooms; and those which directly help the development of physical and mental abilities like constructional toys. By praising simple everyday objects like cotton reels, he leads the way to a whole new fascinating line of thought – is the simple toy a more vivid stimulant to the child's imagination than the exquisitely made and decorated ravisher-of-the-eye like an eighteenth-century doll? It is not only the theorists who support simplicity. The managing director of Lone Star Products, a leading maker of children's guns and cowboy equipment today, has criticized the too-perfect reproduction of guns, saying that the simpler mechanisms give freer range to the children's fantasy. Any mother, on being cross-examined about her children's

Archibald Ormsby Gore, the well-worn
teddy bear of the poet John Betjeman. In
his verse autobiography* Summoned by
Bells *John Betjeman calls him:*

*'Archibald my safe old bear
Whose woollen eyes looked sad or glad at me.
Whose ample forehead I could wet with tears,
Whose half-moon ears received my confidence,
Who made me laugh, who never let me down.'*

6 and 7 Left An English pestle or champing tree for mashing fodder, of about 1800. Its basic shape lent itself easily to adaptation as a doll. Right The same shape seen in a nineteenth-century peg top doll in Welsh costume

8 Albert Edward, Prince of Wales, later Edward VII, posed with a ball — one of the oldest toy shapes. A lithograph from a painting by Winterhalter

9 A few of the dolls from the collection of Queen Victoria, for which she and her governess Baroness Lehzen made the clothes. The dolls represent actresses and ballerinas popular at the time, as well as imaginary court ladies. These four are named Appolonia, Countess Delaville, Juno, Duchess of Durham, Lady Nina Morton and Rebekah, Duchess of Montjoy

favourite toys, will tell you apologetically or defiantly: 'They seem to like such odd things . . . my own shoes and clothes and hats . . . an old biscuit tin banged with a wooden spoon . . . a cardboard box on the end of a piece of string . . .' And what rich godparent has not had the humbling effect of presenting the largest grandest doll in the world to a favourite god-daughter, only to find her playing happily with the oldest most battered toy minutes later, the new arrival totally discarded in a corner. In short, when Cowper wrote:

> Men deal with life, as children with their play
> Who first misuse, then cast their toys away.

the modern theorists would reply that the children had certainly been given the wrong toys – and as for the men, they had probably also been given the wrong toys as children, to deal with life so shabbily.

But the realization of the child's need for a simple toy is not totally confined to the present age. As early as 1812, Maria Edgeworth in her book *Practical Education* fired a broadside at what she imagined to be unsuitable toys in the following piece of imaginary dialogue:

' "Why don't you play with your playthings, my dear? I am sure that I have bought toys enough for you; why can't you divert yourself instead of breaking them to pieces?" says a mother to her child, who stands idle and miserable, surrounded by disjointed dolls, maimed horses, coaches and one-horse chairs without wheels and a nameless wreck of gilded lumber. . . .' Maria Edgeworth concludes by saying that 'A boy who has use of his limbs and whose mind is untainted with prejudice would in all probability prefer a substantial cart, in which he could carry weeds, earth and stones up and down hill, to the finest frail coach and six that ever came out of a toyshop.'

Councillor Patrick Murray, of the Museum of Childhood, Edinburgh, has made an interesting study of 'emergent toys' – the toys of poor children, which they have made themselves out of the material available. One, shown in figure 6, is basically

DOLL A LA WATTEAU
From an original figure, expressly designed by
MRS DAVID and dressed by CREMER JUNIOR

10 A coloured plate given away by the Englishwoman's Domestic Magazine with directions on how to dress the doll, which was sold by Cremers, the most famous of London's nineteenth-century toyshops

11 The rattle, usually a child's first toy, has existed in simple and elaborate forms since antiquity. A gold rattle made for the King of Rome, son of Napoleon I

an English 'champing tree' for mashing fodder, or a pestle, dated about 1800, but clearly its shape makes it an excellent natural toy for children. Yet it is not only the children of the poor, to whom lavish toys are not available, who turn to the wooden spoon wrapped in flannel or the orange box tacked onto the wheels of an old pram (figure 290). One of the fascinating facts which emerges from a study of the history of toys is their extraordinary universality. Again and again, the same basic pattern of toy emerges from among races who could not possibly have been in touch with each other's cultures. Sometimes a toy will vanish for a couple of centuries, apparently for ever, only to reappear in a completely different part of the world for no obvious reason.

The yo-yo is an excellent example of this phenomenon. The yo-yo was known in the Far East in the most ancient times, and in the Philippines was actually used as a weapon, its user hiding in a tree, and striking his victim lethally on the head. Centuries later the diabolo, a toy from the same family as the yo-yo, was brought to France from Peking by missionaries, who knew that the French Minister of State, Bertin, was a great amateur of Chinese curiosities. As the 'emigrette' the yo-yo swept France under the Directory during the 1790s. Over a hundred years later it swept England and America in the 1920s, to the extent that a Persian newspaper wrote an angry leader denouncing this dangerous toy imported from the United States as an example of a time-wasting and immoral novelty: 'This game, like the deadly plagues which used to come from India or Arabia, has come from Europe . . . even mothers who formerly attended to the care of children and households, now spend all their time playing yo-yo.'

An example of the universal type of toy-shape, popular in all countries, civilisations and times, is the ordinary rattle shape. Both the rattle (figure 11) and the ball (figure 8) derive from the simple globular shape of a fruit, nut or gourd, either carved out for a ball or with the seeds left inside for a rattle. The extraordinary similarity of the ancient rattle to the modern one makes it perhaps the most unchanging of all toys. Pope's description of:

> the child, by Nature's kindly law
> Pleased with a rattle, tickled with a straw

applies to peoples as far apart in time and place as the early Egyptians, the South Sea Islanders and the Eskimos just as much as to the twentieth-century English baby. The semi-religious use of certain rattles to ward off evil spirits with their clatter presumably never prevented children of the period from enjoying the noise.

How strange that Rousseau should have attacked the rattle in the eighteenth-century as an article which accustomed a child to luxury from its birth! His disapproval of the rich corals of the infant aristocrats of his time – similar to the later example belonging to the young King of Rome shown here (figure 11) – led him to advocate such simple things as a branch of a tree and toys based on natural objects, like fruit and flowers, as more suitable for the proper upbringing of a child, thus completely ignoring the primitive history and fundamental nature of the rattle. One is reminded of Thoreau's angry complaints about an American backwood's store in the nineteenth century: 'Here was a little of everything in a small compass to satisfy the wants and ambitions of the woods . . . but there seemed to be as usual a preponderance of children's toys – dogs to bark, and cats to mew, and trumpets to blow, where natives there hardly are yet. As if a child born in the Maine woods, among the pine cones and cedar berries, could not do without such a sugar-man or skipping-jack as a young Rothschild has.'

12 The Graham Children *painted by William Hogarth in 1742, a conversation piece showing children playing with a musical box*

The universality of toys may be compared to the mysterious way in which folk myths or religious traditions appear and disappear across the world, showing an identity of pattern, yet having no provable connection with each other. Presumably these toys are the product of very deep-seated infantile instincts, unrelated to differences in race and time. At a recent conference of the International Council for Children's Play, at which representatives from a dozen countries were present, it was stated that in an experiment conducted in Senegal it was discovered that the toys most popular with the African children were identical to the ones most popular with European children. When a play centre was founded at Enugu in Nigeria, the children were so anxious to play with the European toys provided, that they did not mind walking long distances to the centre, and, although restricted by numbers and lack of space to two two-hour periods a week, would come hopefully at other times, only to be turned away.

These universal toys are more common among the toys of early infancy than the toys of later childhood. G.K. Chesterton noted that when children are very young, they do not need fairy tales but only real-life tales, since real-life is to them romantic. It is older children who find realistic stories too uninspiring, and turn away from reality to the romantic world of fairyland. Moreover toys of infancy are of a fundamental and often universal nature, whereas the older child demands something more elaborate, and more connected with the world around him. It is these more advanced toys which are likely to show the natural fluctuations of social and economic changes.

The evidence which toys provide about the economic and social life of their period is an enormous subject, and to many perhaps it is the most worthwhile aspect of the history of toys, since the usefulness of toys as playthings has clearly been outlived, once they form part of a museum or collection. Nothing is more

13 Opposite *Miss Browning, a French bisque doll, with a kid body, made by Jumeau and used as a fashion model*

14 A modern Danish toy soldier made of painted beechwood

natural than that a toy should reflect the life of its period, so that one is scarcely surprised to find knights on horseback during the Middle Ages (figure 68), soldiers at the time of Frederick the Great (figure 116), spacemen or musical 'Beatle' toys with guitars in the 1960s. Ample evidence of the mirror which playthings hold up to their times, will be found in this book.

At the same time, certain toys are clearly works of art, and as such have an independent existence and attraction, quite apart from their significance as play-things, or their one-time appeal to children. This is the aspect of toys which attracts the collector rather than the parent. The collector's approach to toys is most important, for without the enthusiasm of the collector it would scarcely be possible to study the history of toys at all, since none of them would have been preserved! Yet the interests of the collector and the parent are almost in direct opposition to each other, for one wants to preserve a beautiful object for posterity, whereas the other is interested only in its immediate function as a means of amusing and instructing his child.

Nothing is more romantic than some of the triumphs of the antique toy-makers' art, many of which are illustrated here, and their very fragility makes one especially grateful for the opportunity to look at them at all. How well one can understand the dedicated point of view of the collector. Mrs Graham Greene, possessor of a unique collection of English dolls' houses, has written wistfully:

It is an old story and for some a sad one, that in a sense these childish toys are more to us than they ever can be to children. I sometimes think that houses are interesting because they are so like dolls' houses, and I am sure that the best thing that can be said for many large theatres, is that they remind us of small theatres.

There have been many celebrated collectors of toys, especially soldiers and dolls. The collectors of soldiers have included many sovereigns, to whom the model soldier was obviously a symbol of the real armies under their command, as well as an expression of a natural and necessary interest in military strategy. Tsar Peter III, King Alphonso XIII and the Prussian kings all collected toy soldiers. Among other famous collectors were Goethe, Anatole France, H.G. Wells, G.K. Chesterton and R.L. Stevenson, whose lines:

> And sometimes for an hour or so
> I watch my leaden soldiers go
> With different uniforms and drills
> Among the bedclothes through the hills

conjure up a picture of boyhood familiar to many. Sir Winston Churchill in *My Early Life* described how a nursery game of soldiers helped to shape his future career, for his father found him playing 'a really impressive game of soldiers' and at the end asked him if he would like to go into the Army. 'I thought it would be splendid to command an army, so I said "Yes" at once; and immediately was taken at my word . . . the toy soldiers turned the current of my life.'

A collector of dolls may be a passionate student of costume, just as a collector of dolls' houses may be a passionate student of architecture. Certainly the successful and knowledgeable collector, whether, for example, of optical toys, as Mr Barnes at the Museum of Cinematography, or of musical boxes and automata, as Mr S.F. Sunley, creates something which is quite unconnected with child's play yet infinitely appealing to the senses, as well as valuable to the historian.

The adult has a definite role to play in the history of toys, for quite apart from cherishing and collecting them, the adult must supply the imagination and industry to make them. I have always thought that the life of the toymaker, like

15 A wooden poultry wagon, a modern version of a traditional toy from Berchtesgaden. The carving of simple wooden toys in Germany in the fifteenth and sixteenth centuries later developed into a flourishing industry

16 A toy horse from Poland, made in cheese, an example of the ephemeral toy similar to the gingerbread man

17 William IV as a Child *by Allan Ramsay. He is wearing a child's 'coats' and beating a toy drum. A portrait probably painted for Queen Charlotte, in 1767*

18 A group of nineteenth-century toy soldiers from France, Austria and England. From simple children's playthings, toy soldiers, dressed in authentic period uniforms, have developed into prized collectors' pieces

19 The Vaughan Boys *by Robert Edge Pine* c *1780. One child plays with a yo-yo, the other with a whip and top*

the life of the gardener, must have a built-in happiness, not necessarily inherent in every form of creative activity. Some adults become so involved with the delicate creative world of toy-making that they bring to it a talent for creation brought from the normal spheres of their life. Shown here are three 'adult toys' – one a dolls' house made by Lord Glenconner for his children (figures 21 and 22), another, a set of bricks made recently for his children by Mr David Hicks (figure 20). Both show the immense hold which the world of toys can have over the imaginations and talents of people engaged in other occupations.

Clearly the designer of toys is an artist, a creator with a special turn of mind, a streak of fantasy preserved from childhood which most of us have lost. Picasso, one of the geniuses of our century, likes to have toys lying about his studio, in order to seek inspiration in them. Other less distinguished but restless adults find solace in a variety of adult toys, to soothe the nimble finger, or occupy the darting mind.

After all, if children's toys play an important part in their fantasies, may we not suppose that adult toys play an equally important part in adult fantasies? Perhaps the father who plays for hours with his son's toys is exercising an important therapy

20 A set of building bricks which together make up Britwell Salome, *the Oxfordshire home of David Hicks, the interior decorator. The bricks were designed in 1964 by David Hicks for his children and made by Eric Young*

on his spirit – for it has become almost a platitude that the toys which adults ostensibly buy for their children at Christmas time are often bought for themselves. We all know stories of parents who scarcely allow the child to tear the wrapping off the present before masterfully taking it over themselves. A recent survey by a large firm of toymakers established that in modern selling adult patronage, in the sense of adult approval, is essential if any toy is to have a really wide sale. Some of this adult approval is doubtless exercised on orthodox 'good-for-my-child' lines; but one feels that some of it is also due to an adult's desire for a particular toy himself.

Today there is much talk of the growth of the 'teenage market' for toys, and dolls are manufactured with this market in mind: yet it would be quite incorrect to see in adult toys a new trend. All souvenirs, for example, down to the souvenirs of the fairground like the fluffy monkey on an elastic string, are in fact a form of adult toy. The history of toys is full of objects of a grandeur and richness which clearly placed them in the sphere of adult toy, rather than child's plaything, even at the date at which they were made.

21 and 22 Two toys made by Lord
Glenconner for his children, illustrating
the involvement of the adult in the world
of childhood. Above *A castle three foot
high and six foot long. The structure is
hinged and opens to reveal seventeen
rooms, including a Great Hall and a
library with five hundred books.* Below
*A dolls' house in the Georgian style made
for his daughter Emma*

2 Ancient and Primitive Playthings

23 Toy animals are among the most numerous of the playthings that have survived from antiquity. Many of these figures may have had a ritual or ornamental purpose, but others were certainly used as toys. An Egyptian glazed composition figure of a mouse. XIIth Dynasty, c 2000 BC

24 Opposite *Balls were among one of the earliest toys to evolve. On the left are two balls made of fabric over-laid with painted reeds and originally containing small stones which acted as rattles. In the centre is a glazed composition top from Thebes, New Kingdom c 1250 BC and round it a group of glazed composition balls from the XVIIIth Dynasty c 1400 BC*

Which was the first toy? The easiest course is to assume that it belonged to the first child, and as such has long since vanished. It certainly lingers in no museum to be inspected. We have seen that toys, just because they are trifles, are not always made of the most enduring materials, and thus the early toys left behind on the shore by the tide of history are comparatively few and far between. At this stage we do not have what we shall have later – the historical satisfaction of knowing to whom a given toy belonged. It is enough to examine the toys themselves.

The civilization of the ancient Egyptians has bequeathed to us several of their playthings, among other traces left of their day-to-day life. While examining the toys of the Egyptians, it may be useful to compare them with the toys of primitive peoples, historically of a later date, but still undeveloped, and also to bear in mind the toys of the Far Eastern civilizations, where so many playthings have originated. This will give an overall historical picture of the development of toys in primitive circumstances, and the basic patterns which occur over and over again in the evolution of a toy, and will demonstrate the universality of toy types amid the divergent circumstances of history.

Egyptian children appear to have been well provided with toys, including balls, tops, pull-along animals and dolls, which were made from a wide variety of materials, from ivory and gold to bronze, clay, wood and composition. The globular or ball shape being an archetypal toy shape, the ball is certainly extremely ancient as a plaything. Ball games were elaborated as games of skill for young and old. Illustrated in figure 24 is a collection of throw balls of painted wood, and composition made of papyrus and reeds, from the British Museum, which come from the 18th Dynasty and are dated about 1400 BC; they were placed in tombs, presumably for the entertainment of the dead.

These attractive throw balls of the Egyptians may be compared with the deer-hide balls used by Red Indian tribes and other bladder-type balls which were used by ancient peoples. Bladders of sheep and goats were probably used by the Celts in early football games and the Japanese still produce today another simple version of a ball made of tissue paper tightly bound with string. A bouncing ball of beautifully woven split cane is also still produced in Malaya.

Another primitive toy known to the Egyptians was the top: the Egyptian tops were made of wood, composition or stone and frequently highly decorated. Figure 24 includes among the balls a turquoise glazed composition top from Thebes, dating from about 1250 BC. These tops, however, were spun, not whipped; the whip-top itself originated with the Chinese, but it is possible that the spin-top may have derived from the primitive spindle whorl used in simple forms of spinning, and the tops made by the natives of the Torres Straits seem to support this view. Another primitive form of top is the spring top, found in the Massim culture of East Papua.

An alternative theory suggests that tops originated in Japan rather than China. What is certain is that in the East tops were traditionally started by a string, a

25 and 26 Two white limestone animal toys, a porcupine and a lion, from Susa in Persia c 1100 BC. They illustrate how early in history wheeled push and pull-along toys appear

different conception from that of the spin-top. The number of theories about the origins of the top, like the many different types of tops, including the Swahili wooden top illustrated here (figure 28), all prove that the top, like the ball, is yet another universal toy.

Another basic instinct, like the instinct to create a top or a ball, can be discerned in the desire to imitate the pets of real life in a toy animal. Certainly numerous toy animals are among the playthings bequeathed to us by the Egyptians. One must handle the subject with a certain caution, in that some of these animals may have been ornaments rather than toys, but it is surely permissible to see in at least some of these figures a natural corollary to a child's love of pets – perhaps these figurines stood in relation to toys as mantelpiece-dolls do to real dolls today, half way between toy and decoration.

Painted wooden cows were certainly known to the Egyptians, and also simple horses of wood or baked clay. The introduction of the toy horse is a natural development in any primitive culture where the horse is of economic importance –

27 A wooden horse, originally on wheels, from Oxyrhynchus, Egypt, probably dating from the Roman occupation

28 A Swahili wooden top and whip of uncertain date, brought to England in 1914

one is therefore not surprised to find it, not only among the sophisticated Egyptians, but also among the Navajo and Apache Indians, to whom, as nomads, their horses were all important. Little horse figures have always been one of the most popular playthings throughout the history of toys, and there is a striking similarity between the clay horses of the ancients, and modern wooden folk-toys, linked, perhaps, by the tourament horses of the Middle Ages. The plaited straw rider and animal figure (figure 33), actually depicts a mule, not a horse – but then it comes from Mexico, and is made in the traditional manner of that country: in Mexico where donkeys and mules play an important role, it is natural that the mule should equal the horse in the field of toys.

The horse and cow are not the only animals reproduced as toys by the Egyptians. Illustrated here (figure 23) is a highly attractive, pale blue, glazed composition mouse with brown spots of the XIIth Dynasty. Also extant are a limestone toy of an ape driving a chariot, an ivory dog with a gold collar, both in the British Museum, and examples of tigers, cats and crocodiles.

29 *A model chariot found in a tomb at Amanthus, Cyprus, dating from the sixth century* BC

30 Right *A group of Hopi Kachina figures used in ritual ceremonies by the Tusayan Indians. After the ceremonies are over the dolls are given to the children and used as toys*

31 Opposite *Left to right : a small Navajo doll decorated with feathers and ribbon work from New Mexico ; a Hopi Kachina doll ; an elaborately dressed doll in buckskin and beadwork costume from the White Mountain Apache tribe, Arizona*

32 An Egyptian wooden toy tiger with inlaid glass eyes and a movable jaw with bronze teeth. Thebes c 1000 BC

33 *A traditional Mexican toy, a mule and rider made of plaited straw*

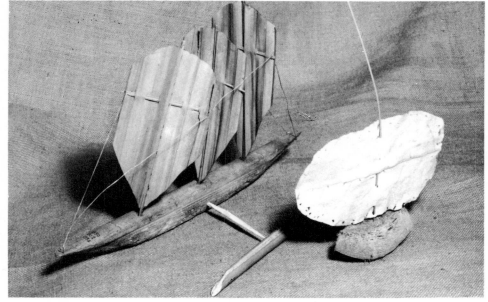

34 *The toy boat was a plaything that evolved naturally among peoples living near the sea or rivers. Two toy canoes with leaf sails from the Trobriand Islands, East New Guinea*

35 A wooden crocodile with movable lower jaw. Egypt c 1100 BC

The next step from the static animal must clearly be the moving animal and the earliest simple shapes of model horses evolve naturally into the same shapes on wheels. From this, follows the pull-along toy, and the examples of ancient pull-along toys preserved in museums are so extraordinarily similar to the basic modern wooden pull-along toy that thousands of years of history seem to have led to no basic change at all. Horses mounted on wheels, having either axle pins or protruding tubs, are found in the Alexandria Museum, dated 500 BC and there is a Cypriot one in the Sonneberg Museum. In the British Museum there is a fine example of a tiger from the late New Kingdom with inlaid eyes, fitted bronze teeth, and a movable jaw which is controlled by the pulling of a string (figure 32). And there is a fine crocodile with a movable jaw in the Egyptian Museum of East Berlin (figure 35). String-pulling itself probably originated in Asiatic lands, for, as we have seen, the Chinese seem to have had a natural talent for devices involving its use.

Toy boats were known to the Egyptians, although, as with animals, one must be wary of regarding all boat relics as toys, for some of them may have had ritual significance. Of course the boat, like the horse, is a toy bound to occur among those primitive peoples for whom water and the boat form the foundations of their life.

The two toy canoes illustrated here (figure 34), one with three leaf sails, and the other with a coconut husk hull, come from the Trobriand Islands, where the boat was as essential a part of the local existence, as the horse is in the life of some nomadic peoples. The great importance of the canoe in the Massim culture of East Papua, for example, is naturally reflected in the number of canoes found among their toys.

With dolls there is the same danger of confusing ritual figures with toys proper. The earliest surviving doll-like figures were probably not dolls at all, but religious images, mainly of a funerary nature, and consequently far removed from the child's plaything as later generations were to know it. The existence of such objects of magico-religious significance has led some scholars to assert that the doll form existed for thousands of years before the first child took possession of it. They point to the fact that no dolls have been discovered in children's graves of the prehistoric period, and consider it unlikely that at a time when men believed in the magical properties of the artificial human figure, mere children should have been permitted to play with objects so wrapped in mystery.

36 *An Eskimo doll from Alaska in fur costume with her baby on her back*

37 **Far right** *A modern Sudanese doll from Kordofan with human hair, a wax face and bamboo legs covered in material. The leather prongs attached to the cord round her neck are probably lucky charms*

38 *An Egyptian wooden doll with bead hair. Thebes* c 2000 BC

39 *An Egyptian wooden doll. Late New Kingdom* c 1000 BC

40 *An ivory figure of a dwarf from Egypt* c 2000 BC.

The *Ushabti* or funeral figures of the Egyptian civilization, are the most famous examples of these talismans, and in the past were occasionally wrongly described as dolls. Scholars nowadays unanimously agree that these particular figures had a purely religious significance. They represented the Egyptian workers who were buried with their master, to serve him in the life after death, as they had served him before it. The placing of these ritual figures exempted the real slaves from interment, so that the *Ushabti*, if not playthings, were at least symbols of early humanitarian feelings.

But if we ignore the *Ushabti* as being purely religious symbols, were there not other figures which combined the significance of a ritual figurine and a children's plaything? We have seen that the same instinct for play and fantasy animates children the world over. This being so, what could be more natural than that certain figurines should have been passed on to children, as playthings, after their religious significance had been exhausted?

The Hopi Indians used to give their cult images to children to play with at the end of their ceremonies. These were miniature dolls, exact replicas of the *kachinas* (figures 30 and 31), the spirits of earth and sky impersonated by masked and painted Indians wearing fantastic feathered head-dresses. There were many hundreds of these *kachina* figures representing the sun god, gods of the warm wind and soft rain, gods of the rainbow and Milky Way, and other denizens of the Indian universe, each with their corresponding doll-figure made of dry cotton-wood root and brilliantly painted. The children were probably presented with the *kachina* figures to teach them the details of their religion, just as a Christian child today might be allowed to play with the figures from a crib after the Christmas season is over and forgotten.

The Eskimo peoples have certainly had dolls for a long period, since ivory dolls have been discovered in the frozen ground of the sites of their old villages. There is an old story known to the inhabitants of the lower Yukon, which tells of a doll-being who cut the gut skin which had formerly covered the holes in the sky, and thus enabled the winds to blow across the earth through the openings. This doll, which walked on the 'path of light' as the Milky Way was known, was supposed to have performed many good deeds, before it vanished from life, and thus the Eskimos showed their gratitude by making miniature dolls for their children.

Max von Boehn, the great authority to whose researches subsequent writers owe so much, wrote in his book *Dolls and Puppets* that 'the genesis of the doll is to be found in a quality shared by primitive races and children', the ability to discern human and animal forms in all sorts of freaks of nature, including rocks and horns, bones and roots, all of which have stimulated the unsophisticated imagination. The selection of dolls shown here from African peoples are all characteristically fashioned out of the materials at their disposal, which include corn-cob, in the case of the Kaffir doll (figure 41), and millet stalks, reeds and clay in the Zanzibar doll (figure 42). Nowadays in India, poor children still make their own playthings out of newspaper and waste products.

Toy dolls, in some sense, have certainly been found frequently among primitive peoples and ancient civilizations. The Egyptian dolls here illustrated are all described, however cautiously, as playthings, rather than talismans, by the museums in which they are lodged. The bright blue glazed composition figure of a female doll (figure 55), which dates from the New Kingdom, about 1250 BC, must have been very attractive to children. A pottery doll on its bed, from El Amarna, now in the British Museum, is perhaps less appealing, but we must remember that pottery

41 A Kaffir doll on a corn cob foundation from Tsolo, East Griqualand, S. Africa

42 A Zanzibar doll made of millet stalks, dressed in fetishist beads and traditional jerkin

43 Nineteenth-century carved ivory Eskimo birds: the bird is an archetypal toy shape throughout history

was not only a natural material for primitive toymaking, but also the one most likely to survive the passage of time, being a great deal more durable than rag or wood. Karl Gröber, in his celebrated book *Children's Toys of Bygone Days*, pointed out that while the great majority of toys have at all times been made of wood, which is easy to work, light and unbreakable, wood is also essentially perishable. Therefore many of the toys which have survived from ancient times are made of clay, or, in exceptional cases, of lead or bronze.

Hilaire Belloc wrote a charming poem about these rudimentary clay toys, celebrating the childhood of Jesus Christ:

> The angels brought him toys of gold
> Which no man ever had bought or sold
> And yet with these he would not play
> He made him small fowl out of clay
> And blessed them, till they flew away.

Since the bird shape is another archetypal shape of the toy world, we can readily imagine the shape of these 'clay fowl'. The bird family of toys springs in essence from an egg shape with a head and tail added. It is found not only in toys, but also in whistles of ancient cultures such as the Mayan whistles now in the British Museum. There are tobacco pipes of Hopewell culture found in Ohio in the same bird shape, and illustrated here are a group of nineteenth-century ivory Eskimo carvings in exactly the same primitive form (figure 43). Clearly the bird shape is an obsessional one with folk carvers and toy makers. Across the reach of history, folk carvers in Central Europe and Russia today are still making the simple pecking-bird toy which gives children such pleasure, consisting of rudimentary wooden birds pegged to a simple platform and caused to move by rotary action. Nor are pecking-birds the only survival of the primitive bird shape in the folk toy; in the Ethnographical Museum in Prague, Czechoslovakia, there are trumpets and whistles in peacock and stork shapes, as well as an Easter toy known as a cackling-hen.

The kite is another toy with a long and honourable history (figure 46). Its invention is generally attributed to the Chinese. Certainly as early as 206 BC General Han-Sin used kites to ascertain the distance between his camp and the palace Wei-Yang-Kong. Kites became the focus of the national sport of China, and with their brilliant colours and varied designs, kites were used by the Mandarins, as

*44 and 45 Antique Japanese ceremonial dolls used in displays, at the Girls' and
Boys' Festivals, to explain to Japanese children the social hierarchy, etiquette
and history of their country. These dolls were highly treasured and were stored in
special brick houses in the garden in case the owner's house was destroyed in
an earthquake. The left-hand group are* hina-ningyo *(festival dolls) representing
the Emperor and Empress and ladies of the imperial court. Those on the right
are* ukiyo-ningyo *(of the mundane world) and wear Edo costumes of the period
1615–1868. Top A mounted imperial guard and two Samurai. Bottom A
woodcutter's son, a boy with a paper bird, a girl with a flower arrangement and
four actors representing the god of the sea, a juggler, a butterfly and a warrior*

standards were used by the noble families of Europe. The kite of the Emperor, for
example, would habitually fly in the air while he was resting. Kites also enjoyed
great popularity in Japan, where they were given to children at the temples on
feast days, as a talisman for the future. As a toy, there is something extraordinarily
moving and uplifting about a kite – and one can readily understand the hero of
Somerset Maugham's story who became so obsessed with his kite that his wife who
destroyed it in a fit of jealousy, unknowingly destroyed their marriage at the same
time.

In China, as in Egypt, the complexity of the civilization meant that toys were
known from an early period. *The Hundred Children*, reproduced in part (figure 47), is a
painting on silk by an unknown painter under the Ming Dynasty, in the sixteenth
or seventeenth century. In spite of its comparatively late date, it illustrates the
universality of toys in China extremely well. Here is an immense variety of scenes
of child life – children playing with drums and cymbals; a baby crawling; an out-
door expedition with the arrival of a dragon and phoenix representing thunder and
lightning, to ruin it; some choir boys singing and acting in a religious ceremony;
boating; boys climbing trees, fighting and hunting; children playing at schools;
children saying their prayers; and finally, shown in our detail, children on hobby
horses and children playing with marionettes. Clearly youthful existence in China
was both varied and stimulating!

The connection of Japan with toys is long and interesting, ending with the
development of the great modern Japanese toy industry. However, toys in Japan
were always far more than playthings, and often formed part of complicated rituals
and festivals. The oldest toy in Japan, still seen today, is the Somin-Shorai, which
has its origins in mythology. It is a simple spindle-shaped wooden piece with
six faces, each inscribed with the words Somin-Shorai. Essentially, the Somin-
Shorais were made to ward off evil spirits, as with so many primitive toys, and
were reputedly made because the family of a certain Somin-Shorai was saved
from an epidemic raging in the district by using one of these spindles, as instructed
by the storm god Susano-o-no-Mikoto. The Yokado temple at Kamikawamura
still sells Somin-Shorais on New Year's Day, and the making of these ancient toys
is rumoured to support the entire district to this day.

In the Far East, as in Egypt, there are early examples of dolls of religious significance, and in the Chinese and Korean languages the word 'doll' came from the same root as the word for idol or fetish. Were these dolls really of purely religious significance? Gustav Schlegel, writing as late as the middle of the nineteenth century, observed that the little Chinese girls never played with these dolls because they were thought to possess magic powers, and as a result he believed that the idea of dolls as playthings was introduced to the Japanese by the Dutch.

But the Japanese doll festivals, whatever their significance were always an important feature of the Japanese calendar. These two great festivals, that of the Girls on 3 March, followed by that of the Boys on 5 May, centre nowadays around a set of ceremonial dolls which every better-class family in Japan possesses, and hands down from generation to generation as heirlooms. These festivals have a known history of at least a thousand years, and beyond that their origins are shrouded in the mist of legends. What is certain is that their beginning had some connection with an act of worship for the Emperor who was believed to have been of divine ancestry; today, the two most important dolls still represent the Emperor and Empress.

Some figures from a Japanese Hina-Matsuri, as the doll festivals are called, are shown here in figures 44 and 45. These dolls have a religious significance and were so highly treasured that special brick houses were built in the garden for them, so that if their owner's house was destroyed in an earthquake the dolls would be safe.

Another typical Japanese toy is a low-weighted figure called a 'Daruma'. It derives its name from the monk who introduced Buddhism to China and Japan and whose legs withered completely away during nine years immobile contemplation. Hence the Daruma is an uncapsizable figure, which children delight in trying to push over. He is also a symbol of Daruma's work and stands for endurance and indomitability of will. Our own modern toys of today of this kind, often made of papier mâché, with weighted bottoms, probably derive from the Japanese saint.

Japanese toys nearly always have a double function – almost every one of them has some magic attribute as well as its function as a plaything. A dragon on wheels, for example, ensures its recipient a long life. Other toys are intended to protect children from childish ailments like measles. Little heads of pressed clay or papier mâché impaled on bamboo canes represent a group of twelve animals, each one designated to ward off a specific harm. Toy dogs are given to women to protect their infants from illness, fish to ward off the measles.

The wooden baby dolls which come from North Japan were laid on the altars of the temple by childless women as an offering to the goddess of fertility. Similarly the girls of certain African tribes cherish their dolls with pious care into later life, as symbols of the children which they intend to have. Clearly among primitive peoples the doll-child connection is a natural and close one.

Nowhere is the universality of toys more apparent than in the history of folk toys, not only studied vertically through history, but also horizontally across the world. The small deviations in pattern in the folk toys of different nations can all be explained by local trends; otherwise they show an astonishing similarity. For example one is not surprised to find a tiger among the folk toys of India, but otherwise Indian folk toys are strongly similar to those of the rest of the world, with the addition of a local jester figure called Vidusha. In the district round the Pribram silver mines in Czechoslovakia the miners used to hold parades with picks over their shoulders, like soldiers with rifles; consequently, the local counterpart of a toy soldier is a miner with a pick over his shoulder, and another typical toy figure is a miner squatting in front of a boulder of ore, wielding his pick. These are the

47 The Hundred Children, *a painting on silk by an unknown artist of sixteenth or seventeenth-century China, illustrating scenes of childhood. A detail showing children on hobby-horses, a puppet show, and a toy drum and clappers*

natural deviations one would expect to find from one country to another, in the general universal pattern.

The Eskimos made ivory toys – because they had a wealth of ivory available from whale's tusks, and were faced with long winters in which they carved toys for their children. Similarly the toys of the Indians of North America, who were non-nomadic peoples cultivating cotton for their own clothing, tend to be figurines clothed in brightly coloured cotton dresses – in contrast to the nomads of Arizona and New Mexico, who concentrated on reproducing the horse. The Somalis, expert carvers in wood, naturally specialize in making wooden animals, and indeed so great is their skill, that what was once a simple art for making toys for their own children, has now grown into a mammoth tourist trade. Nevertheless the basis for it all was the wood-carving which was always part of their existence.

In conclusion it is interesting to observe that where a culture has been transferred from its natural environment to another one for social reasons, the type of toy often remains fossilized in the earlier pattern. The writer V.S.Naipaul, whose family formed part of a body of Indians who migrated from India to Trinidad, informed the author that when the Indo-Gangetic civilization, in whose traditions he was brought up, was transferred to the West Indies, its customs were preserved. Hence the archaic clay cooking pots were used, although it would have been cheaper and more practical to buy the ready-made tin ones in the shops. But Indian implements are always preserved in the same shape as a matter of religious significance, even if the materials change slightly. Consequently the children, imitating their elders, played with archaic toy stoves, while the yard would perhaps contain a real symbol of modern civilization like a Jaguar.

48 A Chinese tiger made of papier mâché in about 1905

49 A Balinese votive doll, about 1880,
made of dried palm leaves

3 Toys of the Greeks and Romans

50 Children playing with toy handcarts on a Greek Attic vase of 400 BC

Perhaps the first clue to the toys of a particular civilization should be its treatment of its children, and the most striking fact we know about the treatment of children in Ancient Greece is that they were on occasion left exposed to the elements to see if they would survive. However, as Sir Maurice Bowra wrote in *The Greek Experience*, discussing the Greek terrain, with its fundamental influence on the Greek character: 'Such a land demands that its inhabitants should be tough, active, enterprising, and intelligent. When the Greeks exposed unwanted children at birth, they showed how seriously they interpreted the exacting conditions of their existence, and followed the example of nature, which exerts its own selection and control by allowing only the strongest to survive.' There is plenty of evidence of the existence of toys in Greece, and also an indisputable emphasis on physical prowess, indicated by those toys which demand skill and physical dexterity and stretch these capacities to the utmost.

The desire for health was inextricably connected with the Greek cult of the body – through their bodies men resembled gods, and the gods therefore guided and guarded development. The new-born child was protected by Hera, and when he was a little older he passed under the care of Artemis, the goddess of all young and growing creatures. To her temple by a stream outside Sparta nurses brought young boys and consecrated them to her, and her feast was celebrated with dances, masquerades and sacrifices of loaves and sucking pigs. The whole process of birth and growth was directed and watched over by the gods, and at each stage it was the young body that called for their care, whether it was being strengthened in the beginning by being passed over a fire, or later being exercised in games and dances, or tested by initiation ceremonies. Health is good because it is given by the gods – the body therefore must be preserved with care. It is not surprising, therefore, to find Greek sculptors and painters taking a positive delight in depicting youthful games and pastimes. Education was also taken seriously by the aristocracy of Rome. In the early years of the Republic, parents took enormous care to inculcate upper class virtues upon their children, and stress was laid on the example of the heroes of the past. In short, in both Greece and Rome the education of the children was by no means left to chance.

Although toys are comparatively rarely mentioned in the literature of the ancient world, we know from other sources, principally vases and reliefs, that the children of the Greeks and Romans had many different kinds of toys. These were made of a variety of materials, including bone, wood, leather, lead and bronze, as well as clay, which probably means that they were intended for a variety of income groups. The references which do occur in literature show that the toy was a commonplace and not a rarity. In the *Clouds* of Aristophanes, Strepsiades, talking of his son, says that he builds houses, makes boats and also little leather carts. Socrates was discovered by Alcibiades romping with his children on a hobby horse, and Horace also mentions hobby horses.

51 A painted terracotta figure of a man riding on a goose. Greek, fifth century BC

But the most attractive source of knowledge of Greek children's toys is certainly the multitude of vases which illustrate the sort of lives they led. In Athens children were actually given little vases specially made for them, decorated with the scenes of infancy, at the ceremony which took place every Spring to bless the new vegetation. At the festival of Eleusis, objects purporting to be the favourite toys of the infant Bacchus were regularly carried in procession. In Rome, toys were used on several festival occasions, and during the feasts celebrated towards the end of the Saturnalia, the Romans offered up baked clay figures which the children had kept for them.

The cradle toys of the children in Rome were consecrated to Bacchus, and at the moment of puberty, the toys and dolls of childhood in Rome were consecrated to Jupiter, Mercury and Diana, and in Greece to Zeus, Hermes and Artemis. In the temple of Olympian Zeus at Elis, Pausanias remarked on a little doll's bed among the offerings to the god. On the other hand, if a child died, its toys were offered to the gods of the underworld; these consecrations may be compared to the votive offerings to the Virgin in primitive Italian peasant chapels, and some at least of them

52 Opposite Children's toys often reflect a nation's concept of a hero, and children as far back as in Greek times have had a predilection for war games as illustrated by this clay war chariot from Athens

53 Below left A child crawling towards a cart. Late fifth-century Attic vase

must have been toys, not purely religious figures, since there is evidence of a known toy industry in Athens.

Animals, whether as ornaments or playthings, played a tremendous part in the toys of the Greeks and Romans. We have seen earlier that where children feel a natural predilection, this will nearly always be followed by some sort of toy, and since children nearly always want to keep live pets, they naturally want to have some representation of their pets, rather as grown-ups want photographs or drawings of people they love. In another sense a toy animal is perhaps a more satisfactory plaything than a pet, for the fluffy black toy cat is at the child's mercy, where the wriggling live black kitten can all too easily escape.

Certainly Greek and Roman children were enthusiastic keepers of pets as can be seen on reliefs. They therefore had a wide range of animal figures as toys. Terracotta horses appear to have been the favourites; but deer, cows, bulls, goats,

54 The importance of the hoop in Greek life, not only as a toy but also as a means of physical fitness, is seen in the figure of Ganymede with a hoop painted on an early fifth-century BC Attic vase

56 A terracotta rattle in the form of a pig. Hellenistic-Greek found in Cyprus. Second century BC

rams, pigs, rabbits, geese, doves and cocks are also found. A toy which Roman children presumably enjoyed was a reproduction of the Trojan horse, which played much the same part for them as a Noah's Ark filled with animals does for us. Perhaps Roman children filled their Trojan horses with soldiers, for there are illustrations of the Trojan horse in the celebrated Vatican Virgil bearing a strong resemblance to toys. Replicas of the Trojan horse were also sold at the ruins of Troy itself, rather as souvenir replicas of stately homes in England are sold by the owners at the door of the house today.

Many rattles among the Greeks and Romans took animal forms, and rattle shapes known to them included owls, pigs, tortoises as well as non-animal shapes such as a cradle and child, or a boy on a goose. Illustrated here is a typical rattle in the shape of a pig (figure 56). Anita E. Klein, in a fascinating investigation, *Child Life in Greek Art*, is convinced that rattles in this period were used as toys, and not merely as clappers to ward off evil spirits by a confusion of sound, for she notes that Philoxeles' toys, including a boxwood rattle, were dedicated to the god Hermes. Rattles were also used by the priests of the cult of Dionysus, but this did not prevent them from being used as toys as well. Certain representations show children holding flattened discs, on the end of long handles, which may or may not have enclosed anything to make a noise – these are semi-rattle toys, evolving out of the primitive rattle principle.

Dolls were certainly known to both Greeks and Romans. Most dolls from ancient

55 Opposite An Egyptian blue glazed composition doll. New Kingdom c *1250* BC

Greece were jointed, fashioned of burnt clay, with the limbs separately hooked on by string or cord, and with a strong resemblance to the modern jointed doll (figure 58). Demosthenes referred to dolls in his writings, and Plutarch tells how his two-year-old daughter Timoxena begged her nurse to give milk to her doll as well as to herself. Consoling his wife after the death of their child, Plutarch recalled other of her pretty ways: 'She used to beg her nurse to give her mother not only other children to play with her, but also other dolls and toys to amuse her and in order to share her pleasures with those she loved best.'

In Roman times toy dolls, usually made of clay and occasionally painted, were common. Rag dolls were also enjoyed, some of which have survived down the centuries, in spite of the fragility of the material. The Latin word *pupus* or *pupa*, meaning a new-born child, has been adopted in many languages to denote the representation of a little child, including the German *Puppe* and the French *poupée*. The dolls of a rich child were probably of a more elaborate nature. In the grave of a little girl in the Prati del Castello at Rome, a carved wooden doll was found which was two feet high and had movable limbs. The hands were carefully fashioned, but the arms and legs were represented only by smooth strips of wood. A beautifully ornamented little ivory doll was discovered in the sarcophagus of the Empress Maria, daughter of Stilicho and wife of the Emperor Honorius, who died in the fifth century. The dolls of little Christians were often buried with them in the catacombs.

If there were dolls, were there inevitably dolls' houses? The experts find it difficult to give a definite verdict on this subject. There is certainly less difficulty with the Greeks and Romans than with the Egyptians, whose model funerary houses provide a confusing element. Archaeologists have exhumed small models of bakeries, houses and breweries near the Nile, which definitely had a religious significance for the Egyptians. I do not think that the child's instinct to play with an actual dolls' house is so strong as the instinct to play with a *toy* – since with the dolls or toys for family, the child is apt to take the whole room for its house. I am therefore inclined to reject the notion that a child would instinctively seize on these models for toys, whereas it might easily transform a funerary figure into a doll. However, the existence of miniature furniture in Roman times is certainly taken by Karl Gröber as an indication of the possibility of Roman dolls' houses, if no more, and we may therefore leave the subject open, in the face of lack of further evidence.

The late Hendrik van Loon said that as a child he had looked at eighteenth-century Dutch ornamental rooms filled with silver objects belonging to his parents with longing: 'Since all of these gadgets were made of silver, we children were never allowed to touch them. We could only look, but that was almost as good as playing with them.' He drew the analogy that the Egyptian children might have done the same with models such as are now lodged in the Metropolitan Museum of Art found at the tomb of Meket-Ree in Thebes in 1919. Meket-Ree, an important official of the Egyptian court about 2000 BC, had them placed there to serve his needs in the underworld. Among the models are his brewery, his bakery, granary, carpenter's shop, weaver's shop and garden, all animated by the neat miniature presences of a goodly population of slaves and other figures, including Meket-Ree himself. There is also an enormous fleet of boats, which is not surprising considering the ever-present importance of the Nile.

Perhaps this is stretching the imagination a little far. With the Greeks and Romans however, where the problem is not confused by the burial models, we are on more probable ground. The existence of the tiny furniture may well point to the

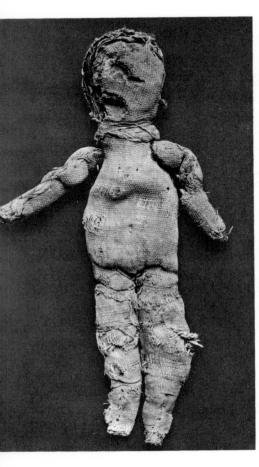

57 One of the few rag dolls to survive from the Roman period in Egypt

58 Dolls with movable limbs evolved at a very early period. A Greek clay doll, jointed with string. Fifth century BC

existence of dolls' houses, and the devotee of the dolls' house will certainly argue that the future architect has always from childhood busied himself with building with bricks, and therefore that the urge to construct a dolls' house is every bit as universal as that to play with a doll. The rest of us may regard the verdict as unproven, in spite of the fact that the miniature Roman furniture in the British Museum is all on the scale generally found in dolls' houses – that is to say one inch to one foot – including small beds, trays, dishes, a lamp and a clay cup.

Where the girls had their dolls, the boys also had their soldiers. The lands and islands of the Mediterranean have all provided evidence of the ancient making of model warriors in metal or clay, and tiny Roman war-like figures have been found in Spain, Germany, Britain and even Abyssinia. A soldier preserved in the Louvre would actually appear to be a legionary. In a martial era boys will inevitably turn to soldiers, and in a period when the Roman eagle travelled so far at the head of its supporters – as Gibbon put it: 'The empire of the Romans filled the world' – symbols of martial prowess naturally became toys coveted by children, who were themselves destined to guard the boundaries of the great empire.

Boats were also familiar playthings. The Greek Empire was largely dependent on

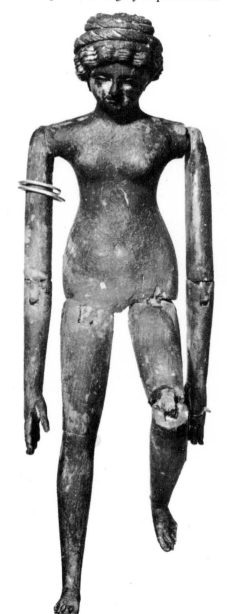

59 A Roman jointed wooden doll found in a sarcophagus of the late second century BC. She has an elaborate hairstyle and wears gold bracelets and a gold ring on her finger

60 A model of a warship manned by five warriors with shields. Greek, seventh century BC, from Corinth

water, owing to its geography, and one therefore looks confidently for boats among their children's playthings. Illustrated here is a toy boat from Corinth, a model of a warship manned by five warriors, dating from the seventh century BC (figure 60).

But more peaceable and domesticated toys were known at the same time. Little wooden wagons called *obuli* appear on many vases, and also two-wheeled carts with long poles and cross bars. On one vase, now in the Metropolitan Museum, New York, a child about to cross the Styx looks back to his mother as Charon approaches, holding the pole of his toy cart in his hand. Often of course these toy carts were playthings rather than actual carts – sometimes they had a single wheel and a long pole and would be used in the manner of a pusher toy, instead of a vehicle in which a child could pull along his brother or his pet.

The instinct to make a pull-along toy is very strong. Many of the horses which have survived from this period have their noses pierced – evidently with the intention of threading a string through them. Others show the strong influence of the market in Greek civilization, and otherwise immovable horses and donkeys have panniers on their backs for transporting merchandise. Even dogs are occasionally shown fitted with useful panniers.

Hoops were particularly beloved by the Greeks and appear on a multitude of reliefs and antique vases. Shown here is a terracotta statuette of a young girl with a hoop which comes from the National Museum of Athens (figure 61). Hoops were popular because of their connection with physical exercise, and were recommended by doctors, rather as the hula hoop was a few years ago, to those who wished to lose weight painlessly – incidentally the craze for the hula hoop in modern times may be regarded as another instance of a toy type lying dormant, but not extinguished for centuries, before bursting into sudden inexplicable prominence again. Among the Greeks, Hippocrates counsels the use of a hoop in his régime, because it promotes a healthy sweat. The Greeks had bronze hoops, but the Romans had iron hoops, sometimes with little rings attached to them, and Oribases, doctor of the Emperor Julian, was sufficiently enthusiastic about the sport to specify the correct height of a hoop.

Like the Egyptians, the Romans and Greeks enjoyed tops. Clearly the instinct to spin something was a very strong one with the Romans, for they had miniature

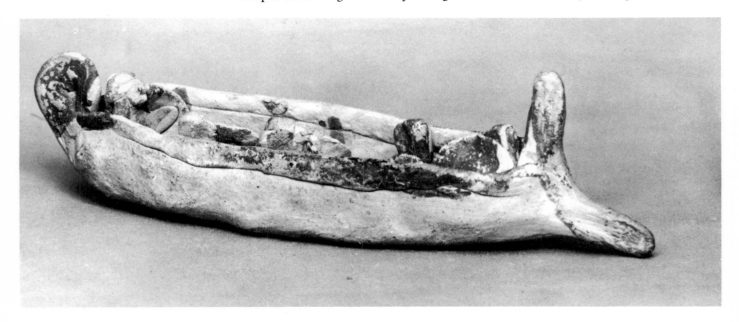

61 Greek terracotta statuette of a young girl with a hoop

tops, as well as the larger variety, and even used to spin money to create the same effect. Pollux described the Romans as constantly spinning money in their fingers.

The use of balls was well known to both Greeks and Romans. Greek balls are made of wool, stuffed into an envelope of skin. They are another frequently illustrated Greek plaything, and it is not unusual to see a child with a ball in either hand on a vase or a relief. In certain cases something like an early game of cricket is being played: a ball is held high in a player's right hand, while the opposite player behind the wicket stoops and extends both hands, ready to catch the ball. Other ball games were also known including one called 'Ephedrismos'. Of course strictly speaking a ball is only a plaything when it is used by children for a disorganized game – literally as a plaything and nothing else. A tennis ball or a billiards ball is obviously not a plaything. But these examples give some idea of the great attention paid by the Greeks to physical culture and the use of the body, which resulted in the natural popularity of the ball, whether they were prone to 'urge the flying ball', in Gray's words, or merely play with it in a more childish fashion.

Another type of semi-sporting semi-toy object which was in great vogue among

62 The Astragalus Players. These
knucklebones were an early form of dice.
A frieze from Pompei

the Greeks and Romans was knucklebones. Knucklebones, or jacks as they were sometimes called, were not only popular as a game of skill, but were also given out to children as a recompense for good behaviour. Jacks are frequently shown in paintings; for example the daughters of Pandarus are shown playing at knucklebones in the underworld, crowned with flowers. Jacks are also represented in sculpture, where nymphs and shepherds play at them in many different representations (figure 62), and on coins and ceramics. Roman bronze coins show children playing at knucklebones in front of the statue of Artemis at Ephesus, and that of Hera at Samos. Perhaps the ancients were attracted towards these outwardly rather uninspiring toys by the notion of fatality, or the contrast between the youth and beauty of the players, and the inevitability of their fate. Since the Romans enjoyed dice, knucklebones and other games of chance, similar manifestations were sure to be among their children's toys.

But there was another streak in the Greek and Roman character to which the grotesque appealed, hence the frequent appearance of masks in the hands of the children in reliefs of this period. Possibly masks belong to the same category as puppets, also known at this time, according to references in literature; but they also belong to a different category: that of the grotesque toy. The grotesque toy will make further appearances in these pages in diverse guises which range from the devil figures of folk toys, to guillotine toys of the French Revolution, to the modern 'weirdie' toys. In the case of the Romans, the idea of these grotesque toys was entirely to make the children laugh.

Contortion and ridicule seem to lie in a border country not far from the land of innocent diversion caused by an ordinary plaything. The roundabout at the fair, for example, is peopled by horses in whose decoration the grotesque mingles with the beautiful and the bizarre. Some Dutch dolls can even be imagined to have a grotesque aspect. In Czechoslovakia the devil is simulated with a forked tail and a pitchfork, and sometimes shown carrying off naughty children to be roasted. A rather cruel sense of humour was shown in the comic figures designed to hold live birds inside them, made in Nuremberg in the Middle Ages. The world of Punch and Judy might be thought grotesque, breathing as it does baby slaughter, violent death and hangings; and the guillotine toys of the French Revolution were so popular that Goethe actually asked his mother to send one for his son. So the Romans were certainly not alone in admiring grotesque toys. However, one may be forgiven for finding their rag dolls, their hoops and little carts more appealing.

In any civilization which reached as high a point as that of the Greeks and Romans it would be amazing if childhood was not allowed its own stream of vitality. As it is, we have ample evidence that children at this period had their own games and their own culture and were allowed their own diversions. Greek life was after all convivial, and although heroic in that emphasis was put on deeds of daring performed by the men, rather than the domestic life of the women, it was sufficiently free for the poetess Sappho, developing her own vision in contrast to the robust, male activities around her, to be able to write (the translation is Sir Maurice Bowra's):

> On the black earth, say some, the thing most lovely
> Is a host of horsemen, or some, foot-soldiers,
> Others say of ships, but I – whatsoever
> Anyone loveth.

This, for children, must have been their toys, as for children all down the ages.

4 Mediaeval Childhood

The golden age of the Greeks and Romans was succeeded by an altogether more shadowy era. In the words of Gibbon: 'A slow and secret poison' had been introduced into the Roman Empire – 'the minds of men were gradually reduced to the same level, the fire of genius was extinguished and even the military spirit evaporated'. Certainly the Dark Ages present an obscure and depressing picture compared to the glories which came before, and with the lack of abundant written records there are no references to toys or dolls in this period.

Nevertheless it would be illogical to suppose that the mind of the child changed overnight and that the infants of the Dark Ages, alone of the infants of history, did not turn to their toys for solace and consolation. Certainly by the dawn of the mediaeval period there are traces not only of toys, but also of toymakers.

However it is certainly true that the position of children in the Middle Ages was less advantageous than it had been in the times of the Greeks and Romans, and perhaps this was in some way a reflection of the sharp decline in the status of their mothers. No longer do we find the splendid masterful figures of the previous age, heroic, honoured and decisive. Women were disdained in principle as well as fact by theologians during the Middle Ages. St Thomas Aquinas actually referred to 'making use of a necessary object, woman, who is needed to preserve the species or to provide food and drink' – and one does not expect to find much attention paid to the needs of childhood in an age when women were so lowly regarded.

Yet the vitality of the child was clearly unaffected. The thirteenth century saw the enactment of one of the most pathetic episodes in the entire history of the Middle Ages – the Children's Crusades. Innocent III, moved by the tales of their sufferings, exclaimed: 'These children put us to shame; while we are slumbering,

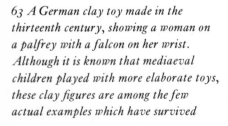

63 A German clay toy made in the thirteenth century, showing a woman on a palfrey with a falcon on her wrist. Although it is known that mediaeval children played with more elaborate toys, these clay figures are among the few actual examples which have survived

64 German clay toys of the thirteenth and fourteenth centuries. Among them are figures of women, riders on horseback and two mythical animals, probably copied from illustrations in the Bestiary, the most popular book after the Bible throughout the Middle Ages

65 *Two children playing with tops, an illustration from a fourteenth-century French manuscript. The decorations in the margins of secular and religious manuscripts, which often bear no relation to the text, are one of the best sources for our knowledge of mediaeval toys. This is taken from the* Romance of Alexander *by Jehan de Grise, 1338*

67 *Children playing with windmills, decorating the border of a page from a French Book of Hours, which dates from the late fifteenth century. The text is one of the Penitential Psalms*

66 *A mediaeval hobby-horse, and a boy playing a fife and drum. These are taken from the border of a French Psalter of about 1300*

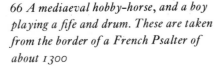

they set forth gaily.' The children of the Children's Crusades were clearly every bit as vital as the golden youths of the Greek vases, if less fortunate.

Since the mediaeval system of education was rough and the standard not high, toys followed the same rather haphazard pattern. There was a total lack of luxury at this time, so that toys were simple and not very numerous. Furthermore, these were troubled times when burning and sacking of possessions was frequent and toys were unlikely to survive. The mention of rag dolls (*simulacra de pannis*) in the *Indiculus Superstitionum* of the eighth or ninth century is significant. A few rag dolls have come down to us from the Romans (figure 57), but, as Von Boehn points out, a rag doll would stand a poor chance of survival in the welter of the Dark Ages.

The earliest mediaeval toys which have been preserved are actually made of clay. The remains of clay dolls (figure 64), for the most part of simple construction, have been found in many graves in French and German towns. The soil of old Strasbourg revealed clay horses and armed knights, and even a lady with a falcon on her wrist (figure 63). Under the ruins of Osterburg, in the Rhön Mountains, toy domestic utensils were found, including an obvious copy of a state goblet of the age of

uia multum repleta est anima
nostra opprobrium abundantibus
& despectio superbis.

loria patri. Psalmus.

I si quia dominus erat i no
bis dicat nunc israel: nisi
quia dominus erat in nobis

um exurgerent homines i nos
forte uiuos deglutissent nos:

um irasceretur furor eorum i
nos forsitan aqua absorbuisset nos.

orrentem pertransiuit anima
nostra forsitan pertransisset anima
nostra aquam intollerabilem

enedictus dominus qui non de
dit nos in captione dentibus eorum:

nima nostra sicut passer erepta
est de laqueo venantium

aqueus contritus est & nos libe
rati sumus.

diutorium nostrum in nomi

68 A tin figure of a knight in armour on horseback which was found in the Seine. Made in France in the thirteenth century

69 A German paper toy of the fifteenth century. The two apes are joined together in the middle by a bar, and when the toy was placed on a stove, the heat made them swing to and fro over the back of the horse

chivalry and a small *aquamanile* in the shape of a horse. These can actually be dated since the castle was built in 1200, destroyed in 1270, and never rebuilt.

The dredging of the Seine produced little objects of tin and lead, probably from booths and stalls which used to be on the bridges. One of these is now in the Musée de Cluny (figure 68). In Gröber's opinion, these are definitely not pilgrim's tokens, but actually playthings. An Icelandic saga mentions a child playing with a brazen horse; and in the twelfth-century *Hortus Deliciarum* of the Abbess Herrad of Landsperg, there is a picture shown of two children playing with figures of knights moved by strings.

Glass toys were apparently known even in the early middle ages, for there is a legend that St Elizabeth bought them in Eisenach and on her return on her palfrey accidentally spilled them. The fragile objects fell over the cliff, but were preserved from being broken by the aura of sanctity of their owner. One recalls the better known tale of St Elizabeth taking bread to the poor against the wishes of her husband. Being apprehended with a basket, she defied him to open it. When he did so, sanctity had transformed the bread into roses.

The obvious toy in the age of chivalry was the horse, or some form of horse toy: the figures of knights on strings mentioned earlier are part of a natural trend. The figure of the soldier saint, St Martin, was very popular with children in mediaeval times, presumably because of his military connection, and riders of fired clay, covered with glaze, were found in the environs of Prague.

In England, the Norman influence after the Conquest inevitably brought in new toys, in a wave of other novelties, and horse and knight figures became popular. It has been suggested that the Normans actually introduced the game of toy soldiers

70 *A glazed clay figure of a knight on horseback, probably made in Germany in the fourteenth century*

to England just as they brought the system of chivalry. A tourney was as natural a subject for imitation in play in a fifteenth-century castle as the game *L'Attaque* was to children after the First World War. Of course, it is possible that some of the soldiers which survived were crusaders' talismans, but from the age of seven boys were being trained as knights, and their minds were geared from their earliest years to martial pursuits. Therefore, horse and soldier figures were the natural concomitants of their play.

War-toys were the natural preparation for the arts of chivalry, just as the Roman children must have learnt the arts of war in miniature from toy soldiers. In the great courts of Europe, most of the man-on-horse figures at this period were made of metal: silver and gold were used, and also lead, which must have made them expensive to produce, and therefore confined to the children of princes, or at least the higher nobility. Perhaps the children of squires and the feudal dependants of the great lords were content to admire or share the toys of their superiors. In 1383 Charles VI, as a child, received a wooden cannon as a present – royal children, above all others, were given war-toys, because of the combative destiny which lay ahead of them.

Another characteristic mediaeval toy, and one of the few which actually was illustrated from time to time in the margins of Psalters and devotional handbooks, or round the ornamentation of a letter in a Missal, is the hobby-horse. Illustrated here are two examples in manuscripts from the Douce Collection in the Bodleian Library at Oxford. One (figure 66) is from a French Psalter of about 1300 and shows a girl wearing a crown riding a hobby-horse; the other (figure 77) is taken from a fifteenth-century *French Book of Hours*. It has been suggested that

71 An English print showing children's games in the sixteenth century. It illustrates a rattle, a windmill and a hobby-horse, and children blowing bubbles

72 Two famous woodcuts from Hortus Sanitatis *of 1491 showing a Nuremberg doll-maker at work, making dolls with movable limbs*

the hobby-horse is actually of Anglo-Norman origin – following the theory that chivalry and chivalresque toys were introduced to England by the Normans, and the hobby-horse was an extension of infant interest in the horse and knightly arts. However, the hobby-horse was known in Greek times. It is more likely that the hobby-horse is another example of the universal toy, making frequent appearances at different times in history, and enjoying great popularity among children at a period when their fathers and elder brothers were almost permanently on horseback. Later, in the seventeenth century, the reputation of the hobby-horse was maintained, and a hobby-horse was actually stamped on a peace penny at the end of the Thirty Years War. Two princes riding on hobby-horses were carved in stone on the electoral Castle at Neuburg, while Rabelais, describing the education of Gargantua, writes of his games on horseback, the horse being a wooden horse.

Another toy which can be found in mediaeval Psalters and Books of Hours is the tiny windmill, which has survived down to our own day in the paper windmills, or windtoys, which children buy at fairs. Henry d'Allemagne attributes the invention of this little windmill to the fourteenth century. Certainly they share with hobbyhorses the distinction of being the only commonly illustrated toy of the Middle Ages. The manuscript illustrated here (figure 67), shows a man in clogs, surrounded by a crowd of children with this whirligig type of toy, and there are other instances of them from the fourteenth century onwards in tapestries and manuscripts. The *Grandes Heures de Symon Vostre à l'Usage de Rouen* of 1508 shows them in miniature; a sixteenth-century tapestry in the Mobilier National shows a little girl playing with one, and in the seventeenth century Abraham Bosse's *Four Ages of Man*, dated 1636, illustrated a child playing with a little windmill.

Rattles and corals, whose influence we have traced through the most ancient times to the times of the Greeks and Romans, enjoyed a new wave of popularity in the Middle Ages, and a special company for making them was formed in France. The corals of the princes are often very splendid – of the same design indeed as corals right down to the present day. Certainly the splendid coral of Lavoisier shown here (figure 75), is a design which could have come straight from the Middle Ages. But the ritualistic character of the early rattle is never entirely abandoned, and corals are often made in the shape of a wolf's tooth, so that the evil spirits can be frightened away. In the royal French accounts of 1390, there is an entry for a

73 'The Seven Ages of Man' from a French book, Le Propriétaire des Choses, *printed in 1482. One of the Ages is represented by a child playing with a windmill and hobby-horse, imitating the lance and charger of a knight at a tournament. A younger child is learning to walk with the help of a push-along toy*

rattle for Madame Isabel de France. Was it for her amusement or to ward off the influences of evil? The Middle Ages, the paramount years of religious observance, were also years of intense superstition.

Other small toys familiar to mediaeval children were spinning tops and whistles, drums and cymbals, and marbles. Marbles came to England from the Low Countries and were known as basses or bonces. There were also larger marbles made of stone or clay, about four inches in diameter and highly prized ones of agate. The hoop was a popular mediaeval toy, as the famous picture by Brueghel shows. It was reputed originally to have been taken off a beer barrel, and afterwards used as a toy. But the hoop was a very popular toy among the ancients, adults as well as children, and formed part of their health régime: therefore, alas, the Norman beer barrel cannot be allowed the honour of founding the hoop. In the early fifteenth century, clay nightingales were sold as whistles in Paris, recalling the archetypal bird shape of primitive toys, and the bird-shaped whistles of the Mayas. The Norman children in England were fond of games, and enjoyed balls and skipping ropes in communal play, as well as games characteristic of the period like hoodman blind.

Were there puppet shows in the Middle Ages? Very little is known of them, but references in early manuscripts prove that such things existed and figure 76 shows a fourteenth-century version. This picture of a glove puppet show comes from the *Romance of Alexander* and is by Jehan de Grise of Flanders, dated 1338. It is probably the earliest illustration of hand worked puppets in Europe. But the general popularity of the puppet show is also proved by the attitude of contemporary writers. Luther, for example, once called the papacy 'a public puppet show' and speaks elsewhere of the 'holy puppets'.

Equally little is known about the kind of shows which were given, because the itinerant jugglers with their puppet shows were not thought to belong to any respectable trade. We learn that in 1363 of Count Jan Blois ordered a puppet show to be given in Dordrecht, that in 1395 a man was paid for such shows and presented a puppet play before the Count of Holland, that in 1451 a ban was laid on puppet shows during Easter. But these are after all sparse records. However, puppet shows certainly existed before the sixteenth century, and there were hand puppets, exhibited in a kind of Punch and Judy show. These fall somewhere on the margin between toys proper and the different territory of puppets and marion-

74 A nursery in 1520, one of Hans Weiditz's illustrations for Petrarch's moralistic work on the Remedies for Good and Ill Fortune

75 Opposite Two rattles. Although these are of later date, they illustrate the type of rattle in use during the Middle Ages which survived into the nineteenth century, without any basic changes

e uoie nel uous toſt ou grant deſtonſiture

A ms nonne y porrois eſtre a petite aleure

S aues ſeignoz ſont il que uous uolons mentoure

S por ce que de noient ne uous uolons dechoure

Q uant uenrois aleſtang trouerois grāt acoure

D epins τ de loziers doluuiers de genoure

M olt eſt grans li herbages que paiſſent li atoure

G ardes ni deſchargies τ point de uoſtre acoure

Q uil na merueille en inde la nuit ni uiegne boure

S e ſerpens uous ittrueuent des ames eſtes ſoure

76 A glove-puppet show watched by three young girls. This forms part of the ornamental border on a page from Jehan de Grise's Romance of Alexander. The figure on the left probably represents Hercules

ettes. But they certainly constitute a part of the ancestry of the Punch and Judy shows of today and the Juvenile Theatre, whose history we shall be considering in detail later. Presumably with their colour and liveliness they also constituted an important feature of mediaeval childhood.

With dolls, rather than puppets, we are on safer ground. The first dolls mentioned were actually rag dolls. The mention of *tocke* by early German writers gives an idea of the direction which early doll-making was to take. *Tocke*, later changed to *docke*, originally meant blocks of wood, and it is impossible to exaggerate the importance of wood as a material in those days. Moreover, the great source of wood lay in the German or mid-European forests, so that those craftsmen in wood, who established Germany's early pre-eminence in the toy industry, found themselves with their material on their doorsteps.

A proper doll-maker is recorded as working at Nuremberg as early as 1413; and then in the mediaeval *Hortus Sanitatis* we find illustrations of the doll-makers actually plying their trade (figure 72). Some of these dolls certainly had movable limbs as early as the fifteenth century, and these early dolls, carved out of wood, sprang from the natural urge of the peasant, sitting by his fire, and surrounded by wood from the forests, to fashion something amusing for his child out of the material available. Records for the years 1413 and 1465 show that at that time there were hand-workers in Nuremberg who made the production of dolls their principal business. *Dockenmacher* (doll-makers), are specifically mentioned as living in Nuremberg, and continue well into the nineteenth century. Even today *Docke*, rather than *Puppe* is the usual word for dolls in this part of the world.

A few clay dolls of the mediaeval period have also survived. They are stamped out quite simply, in order to be easily fired. One from the thirteenth century is merely a rattle box baked in clay in the shape of a wreathed and smiling woman. Similar thirteenth-century examples have been discovered in the Strasbourg clay, and in Nuremberg, too, clay dolls have been brought to light, dating from the fourteenth century. Some of them have a depression on the breast, to hold a piece of money, about the size of a florin, so that they may possibly have been intended to be given to children by their godparents as christening gifts.

What is striking about even these few poor relics of mediaeval dolls, is that they obviously formed part of doll stock: that is to say, doll making as a trade was evidently a feature of the Middle Ages, and by the time we come to the sixteenth century it was of course quite advanced. Dolls are also referred to in literature, as were puppets. Luther, in rebuking female vanity, speaks of woman as a pretty '*Tocke*', as he had spoken of men as weak puppets.

One of the aspects of mediaeval life which brought gaiety into the daily round were the great fairs held on the feasts of the Church, for example, the feasts of St James, St Denis and St Bartholomew. In France the twelfth-century fairs at Saint-Denis, at Beaucaire on the Rhône, at Chalons-sur-Saône, and above all the four Champagne fair towns, became great meeting grounds for merchants and formed points where the North and South of France interlaced and mixed. Elsewhere Bruges and Geneva in the thirteenth century and Frankfurt-am-Main in the fourteenth century rose to eminence as trading points. However the Champagne fairs, deliberately fostered by the protective policy of the counts of Champagne, became the chief emporiums of western Europe, and as there were six markets all told, the fairs lasted practically the whole year through. England too, under the Normans, had her fairs, for even under the Anglo-Saxons the boroughs had achieved eminence because they served as safe places to hold markets. Pedlars also hawked round home-made toys from early times to the castles and fairs, and later cheap-jacks brought them round. The opportunities for toys to circulate were therefore quite widespread.

In all this trading, which made for the break-down of barriers between country and country in Europe, in a way which fore-ran the modern community of Europe, toys and dolls accompanied more serious merchandise like wool and cloth. By the sixteenth and seventeenth centuries, toys and the toy industry have developed into a flourishing trade. By the middle of the fifteenth century there are records of dolls being offered for sale, among other luxuries, on the stalls of the *Palais de Justice*. In a contemporary description of the Parisian scene Antoine Astereau calls them 'charming and attractively dressed', which is certainly an advance on the clay dolls of the fourteenth century, when figure and clothes were modelled together in clay.

At the same time a fashion was starting throughout Europe, in different places, which involved the development of dolls and toys, although it was not precisely in the main stream of their history. This was the practice of setting up the Christmas *crèche*, which according to one legend was begun by St Francis of Assisi in Italy at the beginning of the thirteenth century. Certainly, the saint made a special point of arranging Christmas festivals to illustrate as closely as possible the happenings at Bethlehem, in order to bring home the human nature of the Christmas message to the people among whom he lived. It would be nice to think that this

79 Right *A page from a Flemish religious manuscript of the fifteenth century. The text details the first three of the 'Seven Ages of Man' : Infancy, Childhood and Adolescence. The illustrations on the border show a small child with a windmill and hobby-horse, an older one with a whip and top, and another out hawking*

77 *Children on hobby-horses, from the border of another earlier* French Book of Hours, *dating from the fifteenth century. Part of a miniature of St Martin and the Beggar which illustrates the actual text can be seen above*

78 *Two boys playing ball, with the figure of Death drawing one of them away. This illustrates a favourite theme of the Late Middle Ages, the 'Triumph of Death'. By the early sixteenth century the border decoration is more in keeping with the subject of the manuscript than in previous centuries. The miniature is from a* French Book of Hours

Hec sunt septem etates hominum. Prima etas e[st]
nascentia : Et du
rat usque ad
septem annos

Secunda etas est

Infantia 7 durat. a septe[m]
annis usqz ad quindeci[m]
annos

Tercia etas est

Adolescentia : Et durat.
a quindecim annis : us[que]

81 *A boy on horseback flying a kite, from a German manuscript of 1405. The verse below describes the way in which the 'flying dragon' (*drache *is still the German word for a kite) is to be constructed, the colours it should be painted, and how it should be flown from horseback*

charming custom did actually originate with one of the most appealing saints in the calendar. But the tradition of the Christmas crib is in fact far older – as old as the tradition of celebrating Christmas itself, which was first established by Pope Liberius in 354. Sermons by St John Chrysostom and St Gregory Thaumaturgus in about the year 400 make references to the existence of a crib with figures of the Holy Family, and even the now hallowed ox and ass.

Nevertheless, it was in Italy that the crib became chiefly popular, which may account for the persistence of the legend about St Francis. The dramatic, colourful, and at times child-like nature of the Italians, obviously finds something very satisfying in the cult of the crib. It was in Naples and the south that the crib found its highest artistic form. In 1478, there is a record of a certain Jaconello Pepe giving a commission to two sculptors, Pietro and Giovanni Alamanno, to make a crib for his family chapel in S. Giovanni a Carbonara. The individual pieces are listed as follows: the Virgin Mary, who is to wear a crown, St Joseph, the baby Jesus, eleven angels, two prophets, two sibyls, three shepherds, twelve sheep, two dogs, four trees and an ox and an ass – very much what you might expect to find in a modern crib scene. In the sixteenth and seventeenth centuries, considerable and more florid developments of the crib took place.

The religious fervour of the Middle Ages, which led to these charming cribs, may be contrasted favourably with the crude sense of humour expressed in the comic figures fashioned in Nuremberg. These were built to contain live birds inside them, whose panic gave life to the figures in a series of jerky movements. One feels that St Francis would scarcely have approved of this evidence of the grotesque in toys. Yet both religious fervour and a sense of the grotesque were destined to play their part in the development of mediaeval playthings, just as both these emotions contributed to the panorama of the Middle Ages itself.

80 Left *Detail from Pieter Brueghel's famous painting of* Children's Games (1560) *in which children are jousting with windmills, spinning tops, and playing different childish games*

5 Toys in the Age of the Renaissance

82 An Italian doll of the seventeenth century made of composition over wood and delicately painted. She wears a necklace of glass beads and a cloth bonnet

83 Opposite Charitas by Lucas Cranach, painted shortly after 1537. The doll held by the child plays its own part in this allegory of human affection

'I am called Childhood,' wrote Sir Thomas More. 'In play is all my mind . . . but would to God these hateful bookes all were in fire burned to powder small. Then might I lead my life always in play.' Was he perhaps expressing the strong desire of the average child to indulge his natural instincts for play and to escape the heavy weight of Renaissance education? Contrary to what one might expect, the Renaissance is not a period when elaborate and magnificent toys burgeon forth; and in spite of the enormous strides made in learning, discovery and education, the development of toys continued at a steady pace rather than a head-long gallop. There are no proper 'Renaissance toys' as such. Renaissance portraiture is singularly devoid of rich toys in the hands of children, and royal children like Lady Jane Grey are associated more with learning and scholarship than a high-spirited propensity to play.

Therefore, although there was a tremendous development in the history of toys during these two centuries – and for the first time toys of the period are extensively preserved in museums so that we can see them, rather than guess at their appearance – it would be incorrect to describe them as 'Renaissance toys' because the Renaissance spirit is not one to be fairly associated with toys and child play. Certain toys were, of course, affected by it, such as the peep-shows and movable toys, but these tend to fall within the category of the adult toy. The Renaissance period appears to be singularly lacking in interest in the flowering of the child, apparently absorbed in the flowering of the man. Children's toys at this time are solid, functional and instructive – not soaring and fantastic in spirit as one might have hoped. It is the toys of the grown-ups which show a more florid imagination.

However, this lack of imaginative urge is compensated by a great development in the solid background of toy making. At this time the guilds in Germany were making great progress, and the craftsmen of Nuremberg were beginning to organize themselves a little, to lay the foundations of the enormous toy export trade of the future. No toy regulations survive from the Middle Ages and even in the sixteenth century it is still difficult to discover the extent to which the Nuremberg craftsmen produced toys for themselves, compared to those produced for export. The export trade at this date was probably not extensive, and most of the toys were for the home market. However, the craze for making collections in cabinets stimulated the toy industry, and gradually the pre-eminence of Nuremberg as a toy-making centre began to be established, although all the South German towns indulged in toy-making to a certain extent, and Augsburg and Ulm were also prominent.

However, one of the aspects of toy-making and the Guilds which prevented the industry from developing too fast was the presence of stringent Guild regulations, reminiscent of some modern Trade Union regulations. Craftsmen were inclined to make toys in the ordinary line of their business; chair-makers made tiny dolls' chairs, but did not specifically set up as dolls' furniture makers. Toys could not be coloured by turners, only by painters, and the strictly regulated apportioning of work must inevitably have held back the toy industry at this period. Indeed, as

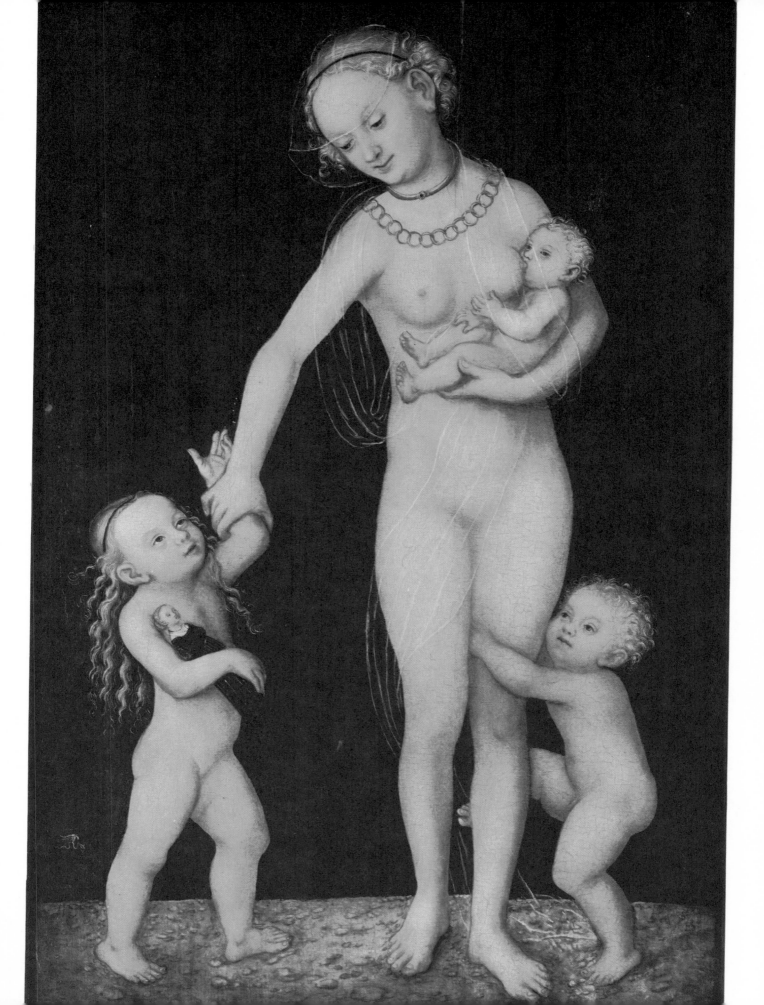

85 Opposite Lady Arabella Stuart, grand-daughter of Bess of Hardwick and cousin of Queen Elizabeth I. She holds a doll richly dressed in the costume worn by Elizabethan adults and children alike. A portrait by an unknown painter

84 An English Puritan doll carved in oak. The deep collar and plain dress illustrate the severity of Puritan costume

the years passed, the Guilds began to have a strangling effect on the South German toy industry, and by the beginning of the eighteenth century in the towns the craftsmen began to be limited to making the finer sorts of toys since they could not compete with the cheap and popular playthings of the wood-carvers of Thüringen, Berchtesgaden and Oberammergau.

This natural talent for wood-carving is responsible for so much of the German pre-eminence in the world of toys. We have seen in the preceding chapter how this wood-carving was a natural consequence of the coincidence of material in the forests with leisure of peasant life in the winter. One may add to it the natural talent of any peasant people to produce a toy which is colourful and attractive to a child. Similarly in America in 1915, the mountain people of Tryon in North Carolina were encouraged to sell their wood-carvings and develop the art by two school-teachers, who wanted to revive the traditions and creative art of the old whittlers and carvers. The young workers used native woods, and developed their own concept from their highland background, making toy log cabins, wood wagons drawn by oxen, and animals of the district; the industry developed splendidly for many years. It seems that there is inborn talent for toy carving among peasants and forest peoples.

The rise of Oberammergau as a centre for the making of light and pretty toys, is closely connected with the carving of sacred objects. In 1681 the carvers of Oberammergau formed themselves into a carvers' guild, not a craftsmen's union as elsewhere, because they felt themselves to be truly artists. One of the specialities of their carvers was a remarkable movable fortress. In Berchtesgaden, too, wood carving stretches back to the sixteenth century, and had reached real importance by the end of the seventeenth century, with an impressive list of things which their carvers made, including dancing dolls, and other objects not quite falling into the category of toys, such as mouse cages, nut-crackers and pea shooters. Altdorf, near Nuremberg, was an offshoot of Berchtesgaden where the inhabitants hoped to supply toys to Nuremberg at cheaper rates because they were geographically nearer to the town. However, their water-colours did not withstand the wet and wood was expensive, so that the experiment was a failure, although their miniature ivory toys are much treasured.

How were these toys, and, indeed, the superior toys of the craftsmen distributed? The toys which were made in such numbers in Germany would be bundled in dozens by the salesmen who toured Europe with them, and often formed part of larger consignments of different goods, sold by middle men, in which the wholesaler played a more important part than the retailer. The agent would have depots in principal European cities, mainly the industrial ones, although in fact German toys were sold in Venice as early as 1566. Royal toys, or toys for celebrities, were probably ordered direct from the carvers or craftsmen, to judge from the accounts which have come down to us, for example the toy silver soldiers made for the child of Louis XIV in Nuremberg in 1672.

But Germany was not alone in exporting its toys. Holland also exported a great number of toys, chiefly to England, thus giving rise to the famous rhyme:

The children of England take pleasure in breaking
What the children of Holland take pleasure in making.

The celebrated Dutch dolls which were so popular in England were in fact originally known as Flanders babies, for the craft of fashioning very simple, very cheap wooden dolls had spread from Germany, and a typical sixteenth-century

86 An elaborately constructed and furnished dolls' house from Nuremberg, dating from 1639, and accurately reproducing the decorative arts of the period

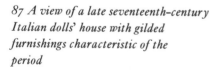

86 An elaborately constructed and furnished dolls' house from Nuremberg, dating from 1639, and accurately reproducing the decorative arts of the period

Sonneberg doll is indeed very similar to a Flanders baby of the eighteenth century. The Dutch also exported dolls' houses or cabinets, and silver furniture, in which they specialized.

In England toy pedlars began to patrol the streets with their cries. An engraving by Tempest, dated about 1692, of an English toy pedlar, runs:

> Troops every one
> Chevaux pour les enfants

Another illustration, showing dancing dolls, tells the story of Italian lads who came to London from Sicily, and by their effrontery, annoyed the local boys, who soundly thrashed them. Certainly the toy fair and the toy pedlar were a feature of English life by the end of the seventeenth century.

But the voyage of the toy did not only extend across Europe – toys were also beginning to venture into the New World. The Red Indians, like other primitive peoples, used the materials at their disposal – in their case, bark and hide – for their own type of toy. But toys were also among the weapons of friendship used by the first European expeditions to colonize the New World. In 1585 the English colonists who arrived at Roanoke Island off the coast of North Carolina, in the words of their official chronicler Thomas Hariot: 'Offered them our wares, as glasses, knives, babies (or dolls) and other trifles which we thought they delighted. Soe they stood still, and percevinge our good will and courtesie, came fawninge upon us and bade us welcome.' Obviously the Indians were pleased with the Elizabethan dolls presented to them, which were so different from their own corn-husk dolls, and bead and feather concoctions. Figure 91 shows a drawing of an Indian squaw and her child, made at the time of the Roanoke expedition by John White: the squaw holds a water jug made of a gourd, but the child, who like her mother is dressed in rags, hugs a fully dressed extremely formal looking Elizabethan type doll.

America benefited in the toy world from the many different traditions of the different racial groups which colonized her. Imposed on the homely traditions already existing among the Indians were the toys brought over from England, and toys made by the Dutch who settled in New York and brought their own

87 A view of a late seventeenth-century Italian dolls' house with gilded furnishings characteristic of the period

88 *A scene from a seventeenth-century peepshow showing the discovery of Diana by Actaeon. The movable figures are set against a painted backcloth*

90 Opposite *A portrait dated 1662, of a child holding a coral. Corals were generally believed to ward off the evil eye*

89 *A woodcut of a girl with a doll and doll's cradle dating from about 1540*

memories of the great Dutch fairs, where toys were crowded on the stalls. William Penn, coming to Pennsylvania in 1699, brought a doll along with his furnishings, a typical wooden doll of the period with slant eyes and oval face (figure 97). Later the Germans brought their traditions to Pennsylvania.

To sum up, by the end of the seventeenth century toys were beginning to travel across two worlds, and the basic universality of the toy, arising from the identity of the play instinct in children all over the globe, was encouraged by the toy's new international availability. A toy could now be made in one country, sold in a second, and enjoyed in a third, by children whose parents had courageously crossed the seas.

Curiously enough a toy mentioned earlier as containing within it a measure of the Renaissance spirit is also connected with the notion of the travelling salesman. This was the peep-show, which in a popular form was often carried round by itinerant showmen in the seventeenth century as a mobile cabinet. Of a more aristocratic nature are the series of stage models in the Kunsthistorisches Museum, Vienna, one of which, the work of the clockmaker Marggraf in 1596, is a timekeeper and a peep-show combined. Marggraf makes use of an inclined mirror to give an illusion of the rescue of Andromeda by Perseus. The notion is actually borrowed from the camera obscura, and as Wolfgang Born points out in an interesting article on the subject this had been known in a primitive form as early as the fourth century BC in Greece. It is mentioned by the Arabian scientist Alhazen in the eleventh century AD and also by Leonardo da Vinci and some Italian scientists of the sixteenth century, but it was not widely known until the appearance of Giovanni Battista della Porta's *Magica Naturalis* in 1558.

This is the period when the blind credulity of the Middle Ages was giving way to the spirit of scientific investigation, and every court of Europe desired to possess its cabinet of curiosities. The Emperor Rudolf II of Austria brought together a museum of marvels which included a number of these optical devices.

Another peep-show in the same collection (figure 88), shows Diana discovered by Actaeon; it has fully modelled figures in the foreground, and a painted background, perspectively treated. This interest in perspective was characteristic of the Renaissance. Leon Battista Alberti is said to have invented in 1437 perspective views to be looked at through a small hole in a box; the scenes were probably

91 One of the first illustrations of European toys in the New World. In 1585 English colonists arrived in Roanoke Island off the coast of North Carolina and among the gifts they made to the Indian population were dolls. A detail of John White's drawing of an Indian squaw and her child, who holds a doll dressed in Elizabethan costume

painted in transparent colours on glass and lighted from the back to show changes from daylight to moonlight. This was the prototype of the peep-show, which at this period flourishes in the shape of these grandiose and princely toys. Later it developed along two separate lines – firstly into the Juvenile Theatres of the early nineteenth century, and secondly into the optical toys which were so popular in the middle of the same century.

Boxes and cabinets, which seem to be characteristic of this time, did not necessarily have to be peep-shows. In the seventeenth century the French produced a number of dolls' rooms. Madame de Maintenon, mistress and later wife to Louis

92 The fashion for playing cup and ball swept France in the late sixteenth century. A contemporary print showing adults and children alike absorbed by the new toy

93 *A group of small dolls from a late seventeenth-century Dutch dolls' house*

94 Opposite *A Dutch boy doll from a dolls' house dressed in the 'long dress' of about 1690*

XIV, had a sumptuous dolls' room, which she later turned into a penitent's closet, when the respectability of her later years induced repentance for an earlier less moral existence. In 1630 a dolls' room was given by Cardinal Richelieu to Princesse d'Enghien and in 1675 a room was given to the little Duc de Maine. These, together with the peep-shows, and the Nuremberg kitchens of the same period, must be regarded as types of optical toys, which gratify the visual senses only, and are not intended to be used in play. The origin of the Nuremberg kitchen is obscure. Obviously from its name it should have been first devised in Germany, but Mrs Graham Greene suggests that it really originated in the Netherlands, because it is essentially an instructive object, designed to teach little girls the arts of house-keeping, and Mrs Greene thinks that the Germans showed an essentially more imaginative approach to toys. Most of the Nuremberg kitchens are about eighteen inches or two feet long and one foot deep, and butcher's shops, ironmonger's shops and calico merchant's shops were all made along the same lines; they were certainly imported to England from both Germany and the Netherlands from the seventeenth century onwards.

95 *The peat attic, a room from the late seventeenth-century Dutch dolls' house from which the figures opposite are taken. Beautifully constructed dolls' houses or 'cabinets' were made in Holland at this time*

The same argument persists as to the origin of the dolls' house proper. Gröber considers that Germany must be reckoned 'the peculiar home of the doll's house', but Holland can lay early claims too, and Mrs Greene believes that the ancestry of the English 'baby house' was certainly Dutch and not German. It is also questionable whether these early dolls' houses – of an extremely grand cabinet-type – were in fact toys at all, except in the most adult sense. They seem far too delicate and valuable ever to have been used by a high-spirited child. Mme Rabecq-Maillard, in her excellent and comprehensive *Histoire du Jouet*, refers to the early richly made Dutch dolls' houses as 'toys of contemplation', a phrase which seems to hit off their peculiar role exactly, and underlines the possibility of a visual toy, gratifying the eyes, in contrast to a sensory one, which can actually be used in play

The first recorded dolls' house was made for the daughter of Duke Albrecht of Saxony in 1558. No picture of this exists, only an elaborate inventory made in 1599 by Johann Baptist Fickler. Many other similar Nuremberg dolls' houses were probably made at the same date which have not survived. The celebrated cabinet given by the town of Augsburg to Gustavus Adolfus, and costing 6,500 thalers, actually held mechanical dolls and other toys inside it. Illustrated here is an early Nuremberg dolls' house of about 1600 (figure 86), and another seventeenth century Italian dolls' house, built on an unusual square ground plan (figure 87). Certainly having a dolls' house in the seventeenth century was a fashionable hobby, and citizens who could afford them, indulged themselves in magnificent examples. Occasionally desire outran the purse, however, as with the lady of Augsburg, one Frau Negges, who so outbalanced her dolls' house budget, that 'she did hurt to her estate'.

In keeping with the passion for richly furnished dolls' houses, was the taste for equally rich silver dolls' furniture. Silverware of this sort was so highly prized in the seventeenth century that it was actually mentioned in people's wills. The idea of silver furniture came to England from the Netherlands, where it enjoyed enormous popularity, at about the time of Charles II. The English, however, never took to it as heartily as the Dutch. Whereas the Dutch loved to have little silver coaches, horses, soldiers, and even acrobats, the English examples are nearly always utensils. Some are intended as plate for dolls, and have initials scratched on, and even coats of arms, as for a real life husband and wife, as though for a dolls' wedding. Certain of the pieces, clearly too big to fit into dolls' houses, may actually have been intended as toys for dolls themselves, according to Sir Charles Oman.

Although most models are fairly carefully copied from actual objects (chocolate pots survive, bearing the mark of David Clayton, a well-known silversmith of the period), there are exceptions to prove the rule. No real-life silver fireplace has been found, for example, although there are a number of miniature ones. Again a con-

fusion can arise because not all small silver spoons are genuinely miniature spoons, many of them being in fact salt spoons.

Silver toys were naturally often given to royal children, especially little pieces of silver furniture. The memoirs of Hérouard, the French royal doctor, record a list of pieces given to Louis XIII as a child, which shows that silver was considered a highly suitable material for a prince's plaything, and the Pope sent little silver toys to the children of John Sobieski, King of Poland, in the seventeenth century, including little coaches. In 1571 Claude de France, Duchesse de Lorraine, ordered for the child of the Duchess of Bavaria a wide selection of household goods in silver.

Having considered dolls' houses and furniture, we must now consider dolls. The sixteenth and seventeenth centuries were a period when dolls enjoyed a great popularity, as we know from the frequent references to them both in literature and in contemporary accounts. We have seen how wooden Elizabethan dolls were among the gifts taken by the Roanoke Expedition to America. The earliest American dolls which the children of the first settlers played with, were also of this simple wooden type. The pioneer fathers, although not originating from a peasant class, whittled them for their children, in exactly the same way as Bavarian peasants on the other side of the world, for like the Bavarians they were largely dependent on wood for the necessities of life.

These early American Pennywoods or 'Peg-Dolls' – the name being the American equivalent to the English 'Flanders baby' or Dutch doll – were not always crude and unadorned. An old wooden doll in an American collection has two corkscrew curls carved down the sides of its face, and an interesting doll in the Annapolis

97 The 'William Penn' doll brought by Penn to Philadelphia in 1699, where he founded his Quaker community. The doll is made of wood and has the typical slant eyes and oval face of this period

96 Opposite *Children at play with a doll, a windmill and a form of bowls, depicted in a seventeenth-century French engraving* Les ages de l'homme

98 Right *The toy stall in a sixteenth-century Dutch market. Among the wares displayed are hobby-horses, dolls, toy drums and bows and arrows*

collection of Miss Alma Robeck is a negro boy with pearl buttons for eyes and set-in teeth, made of chestnut wood, jointed at shoulders, hips and knees. Others have the bright red painted cheeks which have led some over-made-up ladies to be described as looking like Dutch dolls.

Occasionally dolls peer through the records of the time in a more sinister light. In seventeenth-century America, witch-hunting was prevalent. There is an account of a trial in Boston, at which some children accused a half-witted laundress of bewitching them. When some rag dolls were found among her possessions, it was immediately assumed that she had tortured her live victims by maltreating the figures of dolls. She was convicted and executed.

The earliest dressed wooden doll in the Victoria and Albert Museum, London, dates from about 1690 and is said to have been given by the family of the Old Pretender James Stuart to one of their loyalist supporters as 'lately in use in Holyrood House'. She has a large head, painted eyes and outsize, somewhat scoop-like hands, typical of English dolls of this date (figure 99). Certainly a disproportionately large head is one of the characteristics of the English wooden dolls of this period.

Soldiers, like dolls, were enjoyed by the children of this period. Hérouard mentions that Louis XIII sent for his lead soldiers to play with. Marie de' Medici, his mother, gave him when he was Dauphin a miniature army of three hundred silver soldiers made by Nicholas Roger. Later the Dauphin cast his own soldiers, 7 centimetres high without stands, pegged so as to fit into a board for arranging in battalions, as well as a cannon. Louis XIV as Dauphin inherited this model army and reinforced it in 1650 by further troops also in silver. This in turn was bequeathed to his eldest son, whose military education was supervised by Colbert, and the army was brought up to strength by figures of men, horses and artillery produced by the illustrious makers of Nuremberg and Augsburg.

These royal models were developed further by the French military engineer Vauban, who supervised the making of a set of movable soldiers by the Nuremberg craftsmen, Hans Hautsch and his son Gottfried – an example of how important war toys were felt to be in the education of a prince. Vauban's models moved, marched, fired, shot and retreated – all things which inexpensive mechanical toys can do today, but were considered wonderful in those days, when the enormous price of the set, 50,000 thalers, put such luxuries beyond the pocket of anyone except a supreme monarch.

It is probable that this splendid silver army was eventually melted down to pay for the highly expensive campaigns of Louis XIV. It was later replaced by a cardboard one, whose making was directed first of all by Couturier, then by Henri Gussey, who called himself 'dessinateur-ingénieur pour les divertissements, fêtes et plaisirs du roi'. This cardboard army too has vanished, proving that while grandiose armies are the natural toys of princes, they meet the same unhappy fate as real-life armies and conquests, disappearing from all but the records of history.

These then are the rich and sophisticated toys of the sixteenth and seventeenth centuries, including early peep-shows, sumptuous dolls' houses, dolls in many cases richly dressed, elegant dolls' rooms, expensive soldiers and the like. At first there may appear to be a contrast between these toys and the simple tops and hoops of the Middle Ages. But children continued to enjoy those simple but satisfying types of toys in preference to the adult-inclined dolls' houses, so darkly sumptuous and so richly furnished.

Certainly tops were popular in the sixteenth century, and some made of goat

99 An early dressed wooden doll dating from about 1690. This is said to have been given by the family of the Old Pretender, James Stuart, to one of his supporters. The over-large head is characteristic of dolls of this period

100 **The Children of Count Carl Gustaf Wrangel.** *With hobby-horse, windmill and drum the children emulate the military triumphs of their father, who was one of the great Swedish commanders during the Thirty Years' War. A painting by the Swedish court painter David Klocket Ehrenstrahl*

skin were exported from Strasbourg to France. Six types were known in England at this period – the peg-top, whip-top, hand twirled top of bone, pinching-top and string-driven top; the Percy Muir Collection has some fine examples of bone tops of this time.

Little windmills continue to be popular, as can be seen from the tapestries of the sixteenth century, and ivory rattles, often objects of great luxury, continue to be depicted in child portraits. In spite of the new enlightenment of the Renaissance, they have not apparently lost their connotation of warding off the evil eye (figure 90). Hobby-horses still retain their popularity, and the seventeenth-century *Cris de Paris* describes the toy-sellers blowing their trumpets in the streets to announce their passage, and passing by with horses on wheels strung on sticks on their backs – the Nuremberg Museum has an excellent example of a horse on wheels of this date. Puppet shows too, although references to them are few and far between, were certainly known as diversions. There is a reference in *Don Quixote* at the end of the sixteenth century to a scene where a number of puppets were manipulated by a showman behind the scenes, while a boy with a wand stood in front, pointing to each puppet in turn, as he told the tale of a Spanish knight who rescued his lady from the Moors.

Folk toys continue to be made throughout the seventeenth century. There are toy birds, dogs and goats from Kosolina in Slovakia, in the Museum in Klatovy, and a seventeenth-century savings box in the shape of a pig in the Museum of Industrial Arts in Prague. Therefore, although the emphasis in this period must necessarily be on princely toys, it must not be forgotten that the child's need for the ordinary toy continued, and simple toys, even though they have not survived in large numbers, evidently existed for the masses, on the evidence of the growth of the toy trade.

The painting of a peasant family by Ostade (figure 101), shows that a toy was as much a part of a child's life as it had ever been. This probably presents a fairer picture of the childhood of this time than the idea of luxurious Dutch cabinets, gleaming out of reach of childish hands. The child's need for a good plain toy was still met, while his elders and betters indulged themselves in splendid emanations of adult fantasy.

101 The doll seen in the humbler setting of Adriaen van Ostade's Peasant Family

102 Opposite Children's Games: an engraving of 1665 illustrating a wide variety of toys, many of them the universal toys that have remained basically unchanged from antiquity to the present day

6 The Expanding Eighteenth-Century World

With the dawn of the eighteenth century, one is immediately conscious of a change of atmosphere in the world of toys. Now at last some attention seems to be paid to the real needs and tastes of children. Toys are depicted much more frequently in portraits, and the attractive family groups of the period often include little dolls and toys on wheels, amidst a host of white ruffled and blue sashed children. Children's books are on the increase – both the traditional alphabets, for example, 'A was an Apple pie' and 'A was an Archer who shot at a frog', date from the reign of Queen Anne in England.

It is as though the eighteenth-century children at last relax. There is evidence of many children's games and toys such as marbles, battledore and shuttlecock, hot cockles, and hunt the slipper, all of which give the impression that children of this period enjoyed life. Rocking-horses on wheels, made of red cowhide, were enjoyed in England. Although some clumsier examples are known from the previous century, the rocking-horse can be seen as a characteristic toy of the childhood of this period: many an eighteenth-century child, must, in Keats' words, have

sway'd about upon a rocking-horse
And thought it Pegasus.

American children certainly enjoyed the rocking-horse, although rides on some of the early models would appear to have been highly dangerous, owing to their lack of balance.

In the New World there was increased emphasis on amusement, and more playthings were imported and used. The teething coral is a favourite toy of the richer children of the colonists, and the Noah's Ark is considered a satisfactory toy even in Puritan households. The Noah's Ark (figure 109) can probably be traced back to Germany in the late sixteenth and early seventeenth century and Oberammergau is believed to be its place of origin. As early as 1642, there is a literary reference to one being seen on a sign outside a toyshop. But having originated as a folk toy, the Noah's Ark quickly fell into the useful category of Sunday toy – something which could be safely played with on the strict Puritanical Sabbath, owing to its religious connections. Certainly it continued to fill this role, not only in America, but also in nineteenth-century Victorian England, when Dickens expatiated on its popularity.

Puppets underwent great development in the eighteenth century. Characters like Harlequin and Scaramouche were developed, and some puppets were of sufficient distinction to be painted by great artists like Boucher. Puppets were also used to caricature famous personages, rather as nursery rhymes of the seventeenth century commemorate political events so that the nuances of politics long past remain on the lips of children.

Paper and cardboard were often used to make puppets at this period; indeed paper now becomes a popular and decorative material for toy-making and it was in the eighteenth century that paper toys were perfected in Augsburg. A series of pictures were made, intended for cutting out by the children themselves. They were

103 The Family of the Duke of Osuna painted by Goya in about 1786. The boys play with a hobby horse and a small wheeled carriage

104 The Nostell Priory dolls' house made in about 1733 while the house itself was being built. The dolls' furniture was made by Thomas Chippendale, then only a boy apprentice attached to the house carpenter

then backed with wood, and ultimately stuck onto pasteboard. At Ulm, as early as the fifteenth century, an engraving had been made on paper of a horse and two apes joined by a bar, which swung to and fro as the heat of the stove created a draught of warm air. But the later paper toys are of a much higher artistic level, and the paper picture books in the Bavarian National Museum, dating from the late eighteenth century, are most attractive.

Paper dolls were first advertised in the *Journal der Moden* in Germany, as coming from England, and marketed in Germany as being of English origin. In France, the *pantin*, a cardboard figure with movable arms and legs manipulated by strings, became a fashionable toy for adults as well as children in the eighteenth century. The *pantin* was half way between puppet and paper toy, and all seem to have something frivolous and delightful about them, characteristic of the period.

In the American colonies a cardboard doll, known as a 'protean figure', enjoyed a great vogue with people of elegant tastes in the middle of the century. On to this flat card or stiffened paper figure could be attached a series of different dresses. At first they were made about eight inches high, and sold for around three shillings; they sometimes combined the function of a doll with that of a fashion display in a more mobile and economical way than the earlier life-sized fashion dolls, which will be considered later in this chapter.

Cut-out dolls continued to be popular throughout the nineteenth century, down

105 A late eighteenth-century baby house on an arched stand and with an elegant Venetian window. The interior is elaborately designed and includes panelling and a graceful staircase

to Edwardian times, when well-known actresses were depicted; in America there is a further development of this trend. There are a number of paper cut-outs in the Essex Institute of Salem, Massachussetts which are not exactly dolls, but can be formed into them, by folding a piece of paper several times before cutting with scissors. One of them was made by Hans Christian Andersen for the daughters of a Salem sculptor, William Sotry, who had painted his portrait. The Swedish singer Jenny Lind, who had considerable influence on portrait dolls, also influenced paper dolls, and there were numerous paper dolls depicting her during her successful tour of the United States. During the 1840s, paper dolls based on two famous ballerinas, Marie Taglioni and Fanny Elssler, also proved popular in America.

Such was the versatility of paper as a toy-making material that even paper furniture was developed, to cope with the increased popularity of dolls' houses and their appurtenances – in Augsburg at the end of the century, and in England in the nineteenth century, paper furniture was made in sheets, to be stuck onto cardboard for use. Paper ships, paper soldiers and paper cavalry joined the ranks of dolls and dolls' furnishings, and although one might be tempted to put these paper toys into the category of transient toys, the high artistry of the work lifts the elaborately engraved paper toy of the eighteenth century way above the ephemeral paper fairground toy of our own day, immortalized in the song: *I want to have a paper doll that I can call my own.*

107 Opposite The Marriage at Cana, part of a late eighteenth-century crib presenting scenes from the life of Christ. The figures and utensils all date from the same period

Many early peep-shows also depended on the skill and artistry of the Augsburg engravers. The Engelbrecht brothers were especially famous for making these sheets at the beginning of the eighteenth century. The scenes were composed on either wood, cardboard, or stiff paper, and often had oiled paper at the back for lighting effects. The Engelbrecht brothers engraved their work with great care, and produced elaborate and charming perspectives of formal gardens, fountains, statues, baroque scenery. Indeed these early perspectives were of a high artistic level, due to the excellence of the engravers in Augsburg and Nuremberg, a standard which some of the later nineteenth-century panoramas do not achieve. The picture would be cut out on several planes, and with clever use of lighting a delightful impression produced.

Perhaps the development of peep-shows in the eighteenth century was part of the trend for beautiful or simple novelties. Certainly by the middle of the century peep-shows were popular in England at fairs and festivals, and 'a penny for the peep-show' had become a familiar cry. There was a famous toy fair on the frozen river Thames in the winter of 1715-16, known as the Frost Fair, and here the sounds of the hurdy-gurdy or concertina would often accompany the peep-show.

106 The Westbrook Baby House made in 1705 as a parting gift to Elizabeth, daughter of John Westbrook, from the tradesmen of the Isle of Dogs when the family left the area. It demonstrates the importance attached to the stand which derives directly from earlier Dutch 'cabinets'

108 The Ditchley House, submitted by Nicholas Hawksmoor as a model for the Radcliffe Camera at Oxford. The design was rejected, but the model found its way to Ditchley Park where it was used as a dolls' house by the children of the Dillon family

London toymen of this period sold all types of frivolities and elegant additions to the niceties of life like inkstands and powder puffs, as well as toys. Advertisements mix objects of this nature with 'Fine babies and baby houses with all sorts of furniture' and speak of a toyman who 'sells all sorts of English and Dutch toys with all sorts of naked and Drest babies'. Evidently a few shops specialized even at this date in toys alone, but the majority were of the mixed variety.

Baby houses, or as they are now known, dolls' houses, are among the great achievements of the eighteenth-century toymaker; the age which produced exquisite domestic architecture also produced elegant houses-in-miniature. Mrs Greene, in her admirable and exhaustive book, *English 18th-Century Dolls' Houses*, describes the feelings which these charming houses arouse in her as follows: 'It is the home, the evoked dream. It is architecture itself, reduced and sharpened, its proportions bad or good, its fantasies and fashions are here. Walk round it: in it a half-opened door waits and suddenly we are inside. It is the old human dream of being small enough, Thumberlina on the lily leaf, Alice outside the passage that leads to the garden.' On the subject of dolls' furniture, she describes these tiny replicas as 'our own household familiars diminished, touching and lovable, not as we have made their counterparts – the task masters of fatigue'. Clearly there are two points of view to the dolls' house, for it is these very toys which Maria Edgeworth criticized as being *too* complete and therefore not stimulating the imagination sufficiently. I would certainly agree that dolls' houses tend to appeal more to the adult imagination than to the child's – but since toys have their place in adult fantasies, this is a comment rather than a criticism of the nature of the dolls' house as a plaything. The eighteenth-century baby house is an object of exquisite charm, and one is happy that the passion of the collector has existed to preserve it, just as the passion of the contemporary adult created it.

Before 1790, the doll's houses designed by architects were all probably light-hearted frivolities – in England, Robert Adam, Sheraton and Chippendale were all at one time or another involved in the making of a dolls' house. Of course design in a dolls' house often lagged behind the current mode by as much as twenty years, which explains why so many English dolls' houses are ascribed to the short twelve-year reign of Queen Anne.

Perhaps the best known of the English houses is the Westbrook Baby House (figure 106), which was made in 1705 for Elizabeth, youngest daughter of John Westbrook of Essex, by the tradesmen of the Isle of Dogs, when the family left the district. The photograph shows clearly the importance given to the stand at this date.

The Ditchley House on the other hand (figure 108), which is dated 1734, is of a very different nature. It is hollow domed and has eight round-topped arches round the circumference, and is in fact an early model for the Radcliffe Camera at Oxford, submitted by Nicholas Hawksmoor. When James Gibbs' plan was actually chosen, the model was lodged at Ditchley Park, where it was used as a baby house by the children of the Dillon family. It was finally given, in 1913 by Viscount Dillon, to the Bodleian Library, where it now rests, having proved that, although eighteenth-century baby houses may not always have been designed for children, children did occasionally end up playing with them.

The famous Nostell Priory dolls' house (figure 104) dates from about the building of the house itself, which was designed by Robert Adam in 1733. Sir Rowland Winn, who discovered James Paine, and commissioned him at the age of nineteen to build Nostell, also discovered a boy of extraordinary ability at Otley, about

109 A traditional Noah's Ark, imported into Massachusetts in about 1800, but made in Europe

110 A carved rocking-horse imported into America in about 1800

111 *A favourite toy room was the toy kitchen. This example from the late eighteenth century was probably made in New York*

112 *Toy glasses made for the crib scene shown on page 95. An example of the fine craftsmanship that went into the production of these tiny objects*

twenty miles away, and apprenticed him to the house carpenter. When Lady Winn and her sister had the whim of making a dolls' house, the making of the furniture was rather below the dignity of the house carpenter himself, and this job was therefore given to the young apprentice, who was in fact Thomas Chippendale. The Nostell Priory dolls' furniture could therefore claim to be the earliest Chippendale in existence, not so much in the style, which Chippendale had scarcely developed at that age, but in the workmanship.

In Europe, dolls' houses also enjoyed an enormous vogue throughout the eighteenth century. In South Germany they were so popular that the Duchess Augusta Dorothea of Schwarzburg-Arnstadt left behind her twenty-six cabinets in dolls' house form, dated between 1716 and 1721, illustrating the life of the period. They were also extremely popular in Holland, and there are many examples of this period in their museums, although there, as in England, the baby house was the privilege of the upper class, being altogether too expensive a toy for the children of the poor.

In France dolls' rooms, rather than dolls' houses, seem to have been the rage. Some of these were amazingly intricate and elaborate in their detail, and far from being constructed as one room rather than a whole house, for reasons of economy, the rooms would be so richly decorated that they might cost more than a whole house in another century. Flora Gill Jacobs in her fascinating *A History of Dolls' Houses* uses the word 'fabulous' to describe these rooms, and it is no exaggeration; some of them seem to belong more to the world of the toy theatre, rather than to that of dolls' houses. Eighteenth-century advertisements exist for the sale of dolls' rooms. In *Mercure* for 1745 one Raux, a merchant in the rue du Petit-Lion announced that he had for sale 'little cardboard cabinets in the style of Chinese cabinets containing little figures of enamel, men, women, actors, musicians, little buildings of the same material with some very pretty apartments where veritable history takes place' and later the Goncourt brothers tell us that no woman considered her house complete without a Chinese cabinet.

If these rooms are typical of the elegant formality of the French, the American dolls' house of this period, as might be expected, has straight and simple lines, echoing the colonial architecture of the period. The earliest American, as opposed to imported dolls' house which has been preserved is dated 1744, and it is to be found in the nursery of the Van Cortlandt Mansion in New York. It has two storeys, one room apiece, above a drawer which gives storage space for more toys. Under the high Dutch roof with a chimney in the middle there are two further rooms open at the back as well as the front. Although the original furnishings have not survived, there are attractive built-in fireplaces of the original date which give the feel of the period.

Obviously a period which produced so many attractive dolls' houses must also have produced elegant furniture to equip the houses. Here again real masters, like Chippendale, bent their hands to the trade, to produce exquisite furniture in miniature, just as architects produced miniature houses. We have already seen that elegant paper furniture was produced by the engravers of Augsburg. Wooden and bone furniture was also made in Germany, and Nuremberg exported a great deal of wooden furniture, as well as producing it for the home market. Stamped metal filigree furniture was also imported from Germany into England, and to a lesser degree from France and Switzerland. Glass toys, examples of which are illustrated here (figure 112), came mainly from Passau and Zwiesel, and glasses and jugs were made in large numbers, as well as a few chandeliers.

113 A portrait model, six inches high, of King Frederick VII of Denmark, continuing the eighteenth-century tradition of flat figures of famous people

114 *A nursery scene from one of the paper cut-out books popular in Germany during the eighteenth century*

116 **Opposite** *A flat tin model of Frederick the Great made by J. G. Hilpert in 1775 and based on a portrait by Chodowiecki. Hilpert was the first to produce these flat figures in large numbers*

115 *An eighteenth-century cardboard house with movable figures of a sweep, a cooper, a lady playing the guitar, a woodchopper, a woman feeding poultry and also a movable water wheel*

By the beginning of the eighteenth century, toy furniture was sold in the toy shops, along with other fancy goods, as subsidiary merchandise. The earlier pieces tend to be bigger than the later ones. Obviously tin was an ideal material for miniature furniture and once tin was being used for toys, a mass of small pieces were produced, evidently for dolls' houses. But home-made toy furniture existed then as it does now; it is obviously a natural impulse to make your own furniture for your own child's dolls' house – therefore some of the pieces which have survived, made out of scraps, come from the amateur workman, rather than from the toyshop.

The eighteenth century was also a period when soldiers were much in evidence as toys, since strategy and manoeuvre were becoming the sport of every German princeling. The military achievement of Frederick the Great certainly led to the production of model soldiers on a new scale, and the rise of a new fashion – that of flat figures – which began in Germany, in 1775, in Nuremberg when Johann Gottfried Hilpert made forty types of models of Frederick's soldiers, probably in tin, and two to three inches high. These early figures were made of pure tin or a pewter mixture, and the description *Zinnsoldaten* persisted in spite of the later use of alloys. This type of soldier was continued by other makers in that town, such as Besold, Haffner, Statil Gottschalk and Ammon. By the 1790s there were eight model foundries at Fürth, and by 1800 others in Berlin, Lüneburg and Würtemburg.

The Hilpert family of Coburg moved to Nuremburg in 1760. Andreas Hilpert, who was a tin-founder, cast little flat figures in this metal, which could then be furnished with stands. The early examples were signed AH or even with the full name. Hilpert also made animals with Latin names engraved on their stands, and even rococo gardens and sledge parties. As the business of tin soldiers spread, the Hilpert family, however, did not retain the monopoly and other names emerge. However, the particular skill of the Hilperts was in depicting actual people, for example, the portrait figure of Frederick the Great (figure 116). It is interesting that a Bestelmeier of Nuremberg catalogue at the end of the eighteenth century still contains early rococo figures similar to those of the Hilperts, so that obviously certain figures continued to be made in the same mould many years after their initial invention.

At the same time as military manoeuvres were leading to great developments in model soldiers, dolls were also increasing, both in numbers and in variety. The fashion doll, like the architectural dolls' house, was an eighteenth-century phenomenon, although fashion dolls of some sort had existed as early as the fourteenth century, when an English queen sent over to Paris for the latest French styles, thus

117 Above Three Italian flat toy soldier groups of the period made in tin and painted
118 An eighteenth-century German painted tin coach and horses

119 A painted English wax doll dressed
to represent a lady of about 1770,
3 foot 8 inches tall. The delicately
modelled face and hands show the
advantages of wax as a medium

confirming the early pre-eminence of the French capital in the realm of fashion. A fashion doll, generally much larger than the average doll today, was the most efficient means of conveying in detail the vagaries of the prevailing mode.

What were the early fashion dolls like? Alice K. Early has analysed the subject in *English Dolls, Effigies and Puppets*. In 1396 there is a record of Robert de Varennes, the Court tailor of Charles VI, receiving 450 francs for a doll's wardrobe which he had executed, to be sent by Queen Isabeau of Bavaria to the Queen of England. As this was a considerable sum for those days, the dolls were probably life-size dummies, made to the measurements of the English queen. In 1496 Queen Anne of Brittany ordered a large doll to be dressed for the Spanish queen Isabella the Catholic; so particular was she that the doll had to be dressed twice over to satisfy her. When Henry IV of France was about to marry Marie de' Medici as his second wife, he sent her several model dolls 'as samples of our fashions'. From this we can conclude that early fashion dolls were on a larger and more elaborate scale than early play dolls.

However, the sixteenth century was the true age of the fashion doll, when European travel became freer. Helena von Snakenborg, a Swedish lady who rose to prominence at the court of Queen Elizabeth I, wrote back to her sister in Sweden: 'As regards the doll, which, dearest sister, you mention in your letter, we have sent our servant up to London, to have it dressed in the best and latest fashion of the season. When it is ready, it shall be sent as you desire.'

But what began as an aristocratic whim developed into an important part of the high fashion trade of the seventeenth century. Dolls called Pandoras were sent out by French fashion houses to England, Germany, Spain and Italy, not only for details of dress, but also for their coiffures – as in a doll which Madame de Sévigné sent to her daughter. Even during the war of the Spanish Succession hostilities did not prevent the sending of fashion dolls from France to England. The Abbé Prévost, writing in 1704, at the height of the war, observed: 'By an act of gallantry which is worthy of being noted in the chronicles of history for the benefit of the ladies, the ministers of both courts granted a special pass to the mannequin; that pass was always respected, and during the times of greatest enmity experienced on both sides, the mannequin was the one object which remained unmolested.' And in 1712, when peace was still two years away, an announcement appeared in the English papers to the effect that 'last Saturday, the French doll for the year 1712, arrived at my house in King Street, Covent Garden'.

As their importance grew, the Pandoras came to be known as *Poupées de la Rue de Saint-Honoré* or even *les grands courriers de la mode*. The usefulness of having the Pandoras made life-size was that the customers could fit the actual dolls' clothes onto themselves, just as some people buy model dresses today. Marie Antoinette herself used Rose Bertin to dress up dolls in the latest fashion for her sisters and her mother, the Empress Maria Theresa of Austria.

French fashion dolls were not the only ones to cross the water. Throughout the eighteenth century native English fashion dolls also crossed the Atlantic to popularize English fashions in America, as we know from advertisements in New York and Boston papers of the time. An advertisement in the *New England Weekly Journal* of 12 July 1733 reads: 'At Mrs Hannah Teats, dressmaker of the top of Summer Street, Boston, is to be seen a mannequin in the latest fashion, with articles of dress, night-dresses and everything pertaining to woman's attire. It has been brought from London by Captain White.' In 1796, Sally McKean wrote to her friend Dolly Madison: 'Yesterday I went to see a mannequin which has just come from England to give us an idea of the latest fashions.'

120 Le Petit Soldat, *an engraving of 1738 by Nicholas Cochin based on a painting by Chardin, showing the continued popularity of the windmill and toy drum in games of soldiers*

121 *A gold snuff-box with enamelled panels showing the seven children of Louis XV. On the left a girl with a battledore and shuttlecock and on the right a boy holding a whip and top*

122 Henry Darnell *by Justus Engelhardt Kuhn. A portrait of a boy with a bow and arrow painted about 1710*

Pedlar dolls also displayed their wares in the eighteenth century, although in a less sophisticated manner than the fashion dolls. The simplicity of their dress and the everyday nature of their simple household wares, contrasts with the richness of the fashion dolls; their costume is probably typical of working-class clothes of the period. In the eighteenth century they are generally, although not invariably, made of wood; the women wear cloaks and bonnets, and have aprons on which they hold out their trays. Often the name of the pedlar and the date was written in ink on a piece of paper and pinned to the tray, just as the real-life pedlars of the time had to display their names on their licence-to-sell. Eighteenth-century real-life pedlars provided a valuable link between village and village in rural life, and the pedlar dolls commemorate their function.

In the same way fortune-tellers would also pass from village to village, and there are in existence a number of fortune-telling dolls of this period. One fortune-telling doll revolves on a circular stand and when she stops her stick points down to her client's fortune, good or bad. Proper pedlar dolls are, of course, peculiarly English, although many fine examples have found their way into American collections. At the same time the Southern States of America had their own picturesque Negro pedlars, whose street cries were as colourful and famous as those of the English

106

123 Battledore and shuttlecock seen in a painting La Gouvernante, *by Chardin*

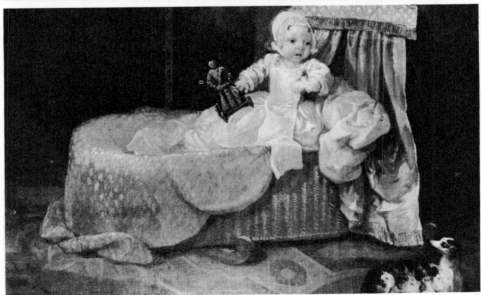

124 Handsome Edwards *by William Hogarth, a portrait of Gerard Anne Edwards Hamilton holding a wheeled toy*

street-vendors in Queen Anne's London. A negro flower merchant of unknown origin, in a gaily sprigged dress with a black linen face, which turned up in Massachusetts from the stock of an old New York doll shop, while not of the same antiquity as an English pedlar doll, is nevertheless an intriguing commentary on this phase of American life.

The eighteenth-century play doll has on the whole a rather stilted appearance (figure 125), yet while the nineteenth century may be described as the century in which dolls, doll-makers, and doll-making techniques came into their own, the dolls which have survived from the eighteenth century are all interesting, and have a weird beauty of their own. Some are made entirely of wood, some have arms and hands of yellow kid attached to the wood. Some have painted heads, shoulders, forearms and lower legs, and sometimes a thin layer of composition gives a glossy surface to the paint. Movable arms were contrived by piercing the shoulder and passing through this hole a little wooden shaft to which arms were attached, so that they could be raised, lowered or turned in a circular movement. Elbow joints and joints at the hip, knee and ankle later followed the same pattern. Eyes were mainly painted with well-marked eyelashes and delicate rather Oriental eyebrows, although fixed glass eyes were also found occasionally in wooden dolls as early as the reign of Charles II. There is no definite clue to the date of the first pair of glass eyes, and consequently experts find it dangerous to date any particular early doll by the eyes alone, because of the lack of certainty about the subject. The early glass eyes do not have pupils, but are made of blown glass with the dark colour inserted afterwards. The early eyes are also generally brown, and brown remained the favourite colour for dolls' eyes until the accession of Queen Victoria brought a patriotic wave of blue-eyed dolls.

As the eighteenth century passes, the costume of the dolls becomes more elaborate, even if the same traditional moulding for the body is used over a number of years. The details of the dolls' clothing, their vests, petticoats, hair style, panniers and neck-lines and the whole trousseau with which a doll might be provided gives us a valuable commentary on the habits and *mœurs* of the century, just as the eighteenth-century rocking-horse is redolent of the nursery of the period, the baby house recalls its triumphant domestic architecture, and its model soldiers the martial spirit which fired it.

125 The relationship between owner and doll vividly sketched by Thomas Lawrence

7 Movable Toys

128 Opposite *In the nineteenth century monkey automata became extremely popular. This example, from the Louis Philippe period, nods its head and lifts the brass dome to disclose three dice which change their numbers. The musical box attached to it plays two tunes*

127 Below right *An automatic toy from Russia. This was carved in wood by a Bogorodsk carver during the second half of the nineteenth century and shows a smith at work assisted by a Russian bear. At the present time the 'Bogorodsk Carver' factory mass produces toy 'smiths' from a nineteenth-century model*

126 This wind-up doll with a cart was made in Limoges in about 1893. She still has on her original dress which is pink under lace with light blue ribbon

The eighteenth century, a time of fashionable pleasure and elegant frivolity in the way of playthings, also saw the development of a different trend, towards movable toys. We, who live in an age of automation may be tempted to regard it as a strictly twentieth-century subject. However, the first automatic toys, and the first use of movement dates from very early in our history. The moving statues of antiquity are no more than the ancestors of the mechanical toys, marionettes and other automata of the eighteenth and nineteenth centuries. These in turn have their part in the early history of automation.

So-called 'oracle' statues were particularly popular with the Ancient Egyptians because they would answer questions, and there are legends all through history of statues and figures with strange attributes. Macrobius describes a moving statue in the temple of Hieropolis, and according to tradition Daedalus made self-moving statues before his great interest in mechanics led him to make the experiments in flying which caused his death.

Archytas of Tarentum, a contemporary of Plato, contrived a model pigeon which flew, and in the Iliad there is a reference to mechanical toys. There is mention of a movable silver doll in the *Cena Trimalchionis* of Petronius, and Aristotle tells of a fourth-century BC movable Venus. In the first and second centuries before Christ, Hero of Alexandria and Philo of Byzantium constructed automata and wrote treatises on them. Hero's book was called *Epivitalia* and described a number of experiments: a bird sang and piped by means of moving water; in a group of four birds and an owl, the owl sang when the bird's backs were turned; birds perched on separate bushes and sang in turn as the water passed into the appropriate funnel; a statue of Hercules bent his bow and arrow.

129 This group of dolls was made by French prisoners of war in England during the Napoleonic wars. The soldiers carved the mutton bones from their meat rations making a large variety of objects which they sold. By turning the handle at the base, the head and arms of the figures can be moved

At the time of the Renaissance in Europe, Hero's works became widely known again, especially in Italy, and not only did his treatises and the accounts of his experiments inspire automata, but also hydraulic waterworks in grottoes, thus providing a link with the classical past.

The Indian fairy tale collections of Somdeva, which belong to the eleventh century, but include material of an earlier date, mention dolls moved by mechanism – one fetched a wreath, another water, a third danced and a fourth apparently even spoke out loud. In 1000 AD the Arabs and Byzantines had artificial birds which flapped their wings. An illustrated manuscript compiled at the beginning of the thirteenth century by the Arabian scholar Al-Jazari, describes the automata then known and includes several which he himself had made, such as two dancing men and a walking peacock. The drawings show that these water-driven machines operated on the same principles as clockwork automata of the seventeenth century.

Research into the mediaeval and pre-mediaeval history of Europe reveals that moving images were constantly billed as novel attractions at fairs. Mechanical

figures would often strike the hours on clocks, and turret clocks are recorded as having operated in a few English church towers by 1400, often without dials, striking the hours and playing a tune every three hours. This mediaeval development – including the little wooden knights jerked by strings from the *Hortus Deliciarum*, which were described in an earlier chapter – existed in spite of the fact that the mediaeval church, so strongly armed in its control over its people, disapproved of apparently magical mechanical toys, as being instruments of the devil, and St Thomas Aquinas in particular spoke out against them. As the sixteenth century dawned, and the spirit of the Reformation and Counter-Reformation presaged a different attitude from the rigid values of the Middle Ages, mechanical invention began to go further.

In 1632, the town of Augsburg presented King Gustavus Adolphus with a splendid art-cabinet costing 6,500 reichsthalers, into which the designer Philip Hainhofer placed a pair of mechanical dolls – a cavalier and his lady holding each other's hands ready to dance by means of an interior mechanism. Both were sumptuously dressed, with plentiful silver braid on their silken clothes, and were almost

*131 An acrobat in a gold costume made by
Decamp of Paris in the nineteenth century*

*132 A black-and-white minstrel made by
Jean Roullet of Paris in 1890*

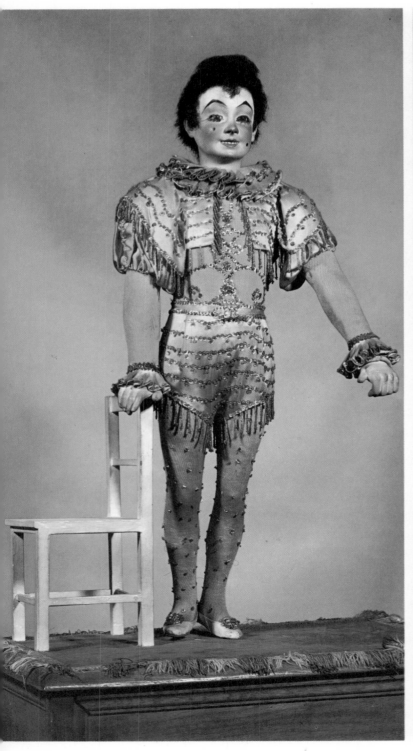

certainly the best that Germany could provide in the way of dolls at this date.

The Italian mathematician Junellus Turrianus delighted the Emperor Charles V by sending wooden sparrows into the king's chamber 'which did fly about there and returned with such marvellous artifice that the superior of the order of St Jerome, being unskilled in mathematics, suspected it for witchcraft' – as described in William Turner's *A Complete History*, published in 1697. Turrianus' experiments with flying birds were part of the general Renaissance yearning to create machines of flight, initiated by the experiments of Leonardo da Vinci. Leonardo also constructed a lion automaton which he presented to Francis I.

Also in the seventeenth century, Father Gabriel da Magalhães, a Jesuit priest going to China, brought a magical walking figure to the Emperor Kang'hi. Louis XIV was given a miniature carriage by Dr Camus, an associate of the French Academy of Sciences. Drawn by a team of horses, it had a coachman, a footman, a page and a lady passenger. When Dr Camus arrived with it at the palace, he placed it at one end of a long table, and set it in motion for the pleasure of the King and his Court. The story goes that when the coachman cracked his whip the horses moved forward so realistically that the children present sprang back in fear, for they believed the tiny animals were alive. When the carriage had travelled the length of the table, the horses made a sharp turn and continued until they arrived in front of the King, where they halted. Then the footman and page stepped down, opening the carriage door so that the lady could alight to curtsy and present a petition to the astonished King. After waiting a moment, she curtsied again and re-entered the carriage, the servants resumed their positions, and the vehicle moved on. Certainly, in all these early and historic automata, jewels were used in profusion, and the richness of the material vied with the exquisiteness of the craftsmanship.

The eighteenth and nineteenth centuries can, however, be regarded as the heyday of fine automata. From the beginning of this period onwards there are striking and ingenious developments in this field. Early in the century a well-known Viennese preacher, Abraham a Sancta Clara, spoke of 'dolls so ingeniously contrived that on being pulled pressed or wound up they become animated and move by themselves as desired', and Corvinus described in 1716, 'the costly and ingenious dolls which display *actiones* by means of concealed clockwork', then the speciality of Augsburg and Nuremburg, 'which are rapidly filling the world with them'. This

133 An early musical box which is a miniature reproduction in bone of the house in which Franz Schubert lived and worked. It was presented to Schubert by his devoted friend, Johann Michael Vogel, in 1825. The roof lifts to disclose an ink pot, quill holder and sand container. A musical movement, fitted later, now plays Schubert's Ave Maria

134 *A group of musicians made by the celebrated Jaquet-Droz family of Geneva in the early nineteenth century*

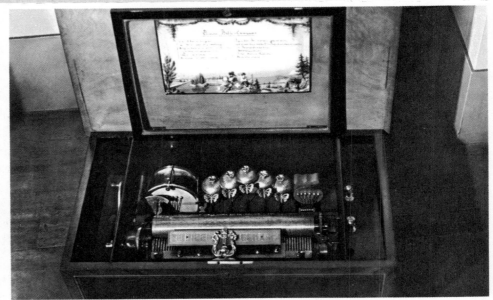

135 *A nineteenth-century example of the musical box which has a choice of twelve tunes. In addition to the usual comb, this musical box has a set of five bells, which are operated by pins on a rotating cylinder*

136 A group of mechanical dolls made in France in about 1860. When wound up, the little girl on the right blows bubbles, the negro smokes a pipe, the girl on the left lifts the lid of her basket to reveal her shells, and the lady on the far left lifts the lid of her basket which contains a baby lamb

type of movable doll which was known as *la jolie catin*, was shown in the streets of France by itinerant girl-sellers, and was illustrated as a familiar sight at this time in the *Cris de Paris*.

Legend has it that the philosopher Descartes built a mechanical figure of a young girl which he called *Ma Fille Franchina*, to prove his theory that all animals, including man, were merely highly developed machines. Shortly after he had finished his model, Descartes took her with him on a sea voyage, during which the ship's captain accidentally set her in motion, and was so astonished when she moved, that he threw her overboard, convinced that she was an invention of the devil.

There were a number of masters of the art: pre-eminent among these was Jacques de Vaucanson, who was born in Grenoble in 1709, and died in 1782. From 1738 onwards, his output of automata was truly prodigious. His creations became world-famous, and were exhibited, among other places, at the Haymarket Opera House in London, while in 1752 the silversmith Du Moulin travelled all over Europe with copies of automata made by him, as far even as St Petersburg. His automata included a flute player with a repertoire of twelve tunes, and a duck whose structure was anatomically entirely correct, and whose every bone executed its proper movements, as well as being able to quack in a most life-like manner; moreover, when corn was thrown in front of it, it stretched out its neck, swallowed it, digested it by means of a chemical solution inside, and finally discharged it in true biological fashion!

Next came the family of Jaquet-Droz; the father, Pierre Jaquet-Droz, and his son, Henri Louis. Pierre Jaquet-Droz's parents had planned for their son to be a preacher, but while on holiday from his theological school he visited his sister, who was married to a watch maker, and became so fascinated by mechanics that he forsook religion. In 1752 he made his first automaton, a singing bird, so tiny that it popped out of a gold snuff box when the lid was lifted. In 1760 Pierre Jaquet-Droz made a child-doll said to be capable of writing a letter of fifty words or so called *The Young Writer*; in 1773 Henri Louis Jaquet-Droz made two famous figures, one called *The Designer*, which could draw, and is said to have sketched a portrait of Queen Marie Antoinette in her presence, and the other called *La Musicienne*, once the property of the Queen, now in the Museum of Neuchatel in Switzerland, which plays the tunes of the Queen's favourite composer, Gluck. When Henri

137 A performing monkey from America, made in the eighteenth or nineteenth century. The monkey is carved in wood and has movable parts which enable him to perform acrobatics at the end of his stick

Jaquet-Droz took control of the family business, he opened a branch in London, where his prestige was such that he was received by George III. The mechanical toys which the Jaquet-Droz family made for the King of Spain were so fabulous that the toymakers were actually in danger of being condemned as sorcerers by the Spanish Inquisition. Among the toys they created for him was a sheep which bleated in a life-like manner, and a dog guarding a basket of fruit, which began to bark when the fruit was taken away.

Another talented family in the sphere of automata were the Maillardets, and the mechanical writer made by Henri Maillardet which is now lodged in the Research Museum of Philadelphia, can actually write little rhymes in both English and French. A further skilled inventor was Wolfgang von Kempelen, who made a speaking automaton in 1778, and a celebrated 'automatic' chess-player in 1769, against which Napoleon is supposed to have played a game of chess in 1809 and lost. Perhaps the chess-player should not properly be included among true automata, for its secret, which baffled observers, was to conceal a well-trained boy inside the box on which it was mounted, who was able to watch the moves made by his opponent in a series of mirrors. This was revealed in 1789 in a book published in Dresden, which gave away the hoax.

The examples of mechanical invention known at this time are indeed many and varied, and include such charming fancies as the automatic group made for Tippoo Sahib, the highly anglo-phobe Sultan of Mysore, which consisted of a life-sized tiger rushing to devour an Englishman in uniform. Although water, wind, mercury and clockwork were the only materials known to designers, they made full use of them, to the extent that even Italian and Austrian peasants made automatic crib scenes where the background figures to the Holy Family could be seen tapping, hammering, buying and selling.

Numbers of craftsmen were working in England under the Georges and produced skilful animated figures and various types of musical automata. Christopher Pinchbeck, for example, advertised in 1721 in *Applebee's Weekly Journal* that he made 'musical Automata or Instruments of themselves to play exceeding well on the Flute, Flaggelet or Organ, sets of Country Dances, Minuets, Jiggs, and Opera Tunes, or the most perfect imitation of the Aviary of Birds'. As Pinchbeck was an eminent organ builder, the music probably emanated from miniature organs.

James Cox was another celebrated automaton maker, who worked in London, and when he held an Exhibition in the Spring Gardens in 1773, visitors were charged as much as half a guinea to view his collection of clocks, singing birds and mechanical toys. From the middle 1760s the East India Company gave him lavish commissions for gold and jewelled automata which they presented to eastern potentates, and in 1766 Cox made a golden chariot for the Emperor of China. So highly was Cox's work esteemed at the courts of China and Russia that by 1790 he had even established workshops in Canton.

Francis Magniac, a contemporary of Cox's, also produced jewelled automata for eastern potentates – his mechanisms being considered to be more complicated than those of his rival. His triumphs included parading soldiers, musicians with their instruments, moving birds and animals and bells and chimes producing musical tunes.

In the nineteenth century monkey automata became extremely popular, and a whole series of them were made from the 1850s onwards (figure 128). Monkeys dressed in scarlet tunics and plumed hats were particularly desirable, and there is an excellent example in the collection of Mr Jack Barnett of Tettenhall, Staffordshire,

138 Above *An oriental ivory acrobat made in the mid-nineteenth century and probably from Japan*

139 Above right *A gypsy girl who plays a tambourine. Made by H. Vichy of Paris about 1900*

in which the monkey actually puffs at a cigarette. Some of the monkeys were as much as two feet high, and were usually modelled in papier mâché. Monkey orchestras were considered to be especially delightful with a monkey conductor to lead the band. A monkey magician, such as that illustrated here, was another fashionable craze – as though there was something irresistibly comic in the idea of the lively monkey with its energy harnessed to the framework of an automaton.

One of the problems about automata was that they were extremely expensive to produce, by their very nature a luxury toy for the prince or potentate, and did nothing to satisfy the desire of the ordinary person for a movable plaything. It is true that there were some examples of simple moving toys in the eighteenth century. In England there were 'bristle' dolls; these were small harpsichord dolls, with a bunch of bristle or brush hidden under their long skirts. They would be placed on the harpsichord, and when the ladies tapped the keys, the vibrations caused them to dance. The same principle is still used in dolls today which 'dance' to the gramophone, and there is a modern American version called 'Microphone Sam' who tap-dances when any noise is made in front of the microphone.

140 A collection of nineteenth century automatons. From left to right: a walking doll from France, c 1870; a running duck who flaps its wings, probably English, c 1870, shown with the original box and priced at ninepence three farthings; a hopping frog; a running mouse; a billiards player who really pots the shots, the balls returning to the player up a moving belt; Mrs Mop, probably English; and the man who rolls barrels along the floor

England also provides examples of the famous 'tilting doll' which had originally come from China, where it was known as 'Stand up, little priest'. Tilting dolls were sometimes known as Fanny Royds; there is a reference in the Creevey Papers to the unfortunate Queen Caroline, estranged wife of George IV: 'I had been taught to believe that she was as much improved in looks as in dignity of manners: it is therefore with much pain I am obliged to observe that the nearest resemblance I can recollect to this much injured princess is a toy which you used to call Fanny Royds.'

In the nineteenth century, the desire for inexpensive mechanical toys was more urgent and therefore inevitably more easily gratified. Early in the century a number of simple mechanical toys, said to have been made by a French sailor called Cruchet, were distributed by the Empress Josephine to war widows who came to her palace seeking pensions. The Empress was obviously fascinated by automata, for among other toys she gave her grandchildren (who included the future Emperor Napoleon III) were little golden hens which actually laid silver eggs.

Many different types of toys of movement begin to be developed in the same period – for example, a sand motor begins to be used in toys. The collection of

141 *A handmade sand-toy of about 1850–70; the product of the nineteenth century desire for inexpensive mechanical toys led to the handmade sand-toy. Printed sheets with instructions were bought and cut out and stuck together at home. The box-back of the frame has a quantity of fine silver sand in the base. By turning the whole thing clockwise several times the sand is guided to a shelf at the top of the box and then trickles through two holes on to tiny replicas of water-mill wheels. One of these animates the arm of the organ-grinder, the other causes the monkey to dance*

142 *Another sand-toy. The trickling sand causes the monkey's arm to move up and down to feed the kitten.*

Percy Muir contains three fine examples in which the sand is used to trickle through apertures on the hour-glass pattern, to set figures in motion (figures 141 and 142).

A natural trend, which resulted in the production of some excellent automatic toys, was the making of things for children by experts in other fields. In early nineteenth-century America, some tinsmiths made walking figures with loosely riveted joints. Clockmakers spent their spare time constructing simple mechanical toys on which figures moved as a crank was turned. Sometimes these included a music maker in the base, like that said to have been made by a Pennsylvanian, Andrew Ellicott, who supposedly put it together hurriedly to amuse his children, while he was working on his famous four-faced clock. The youngsters were so fascinated by the clock's intricate mechanism that they pestered Ellicott, who decided that the only way to get rid of them was to make something intricate and pleasurable which they could concentrate on. A few American clockmakers constructed bird-cage music boxes, complete with warbling bird, although most of these elaborate playthings were imported from Europe. For those today who wish to acquire or inspect a fabulous collection of automata and musical boxes the London shop of Mr S.F. Sunley provides a treasure house of objects from the past: two of his automata are shown here in colour (figures 131 and 132).

The celebrated doll-makers of the nineteenth century, discussed in a later chapter, often collaborated in the production of mechanical devices which were put inside their dolls and operated like musical boxes. Also Jumeau dolls in particular are found on a great quantity of musical boxes, the boxes being clearly of Swiss or German origin, while the dolls are clearly French. One musical Jumeau doll in the collection of Mrs Grant J. Holt in the United States holds a bird cage in its hand, and when the music plays, the bird moves about in its cage, as if singing, while the doll's head moves from side to side and its free hand up and down. Another musical doll in the Holt collection is a boy doll, who moves to and fro as the music plays and puts a cigarette back and forward from his mouth, while his head tilts back as if smoking A little girl teases a kitten at her feet with a piece of string with one hand and brings her doll to her face to kiss it with the other.

Another type of musical doll, known as a poupard, consists of a richly dressed doll, mounted on a stick, and when the stick is twirled round a tune is played. These poupards date from the late nineteenth and early twentieth century. But music is not the only type of automation which was combined with a toy in the nineteenth century. Walking toys have a long history. They first appeared in Paris as early as 1836, and leading doll-makers were eager to take advantage of the novelty; in 1849 a doll appeared with an internal organ which allowed its body to move backward, forward and sideways; and in the 1870s Jumeau produced the Jumeau 'walking doll' (figure 203). At the Paris Exhibition of 1844 Monsieur Brouillet exhibited dolls which could stand up on their own, if not walk, and at the same Exhibition of 1852 dolls were shown which could actually dance the polka.

But perhaps the most famous nineteenth-century walking doll, from the point of view of collectors, was patented in the United States in 1862. This was the 'Autoperipatetikos' walking doll, which had legs with metal feet that worked by an alternating cant movement when it was wound up. Another type of American walking doll on the market at this time did not need to be wound up at all; she pushed a small cart in front of her and while her head and hands were made of papier mâché, the rest of her was made of metal. She was started on level ground

143 A French automaton 'Rose Doll' of about 1860, with a fine porcelain head and hands. Operated by clockwork, she rises from the heart of the rose, looks from side to side, and descends again into the rose which closes over her

with a little push and moved forward by means of tiny prongs which caught in the hairs of the carpet.

The first speaking dolls made in any quantity were made in the 1820s by Johann Maelzel, the inventor of the metronome for the piano. A children's periodical *Le Bon Genre*, from which figure 165 is taken, reports that at the Exhibition of French Industry in 1823 there were dolls which said 'Maman' when their right hands were raised to shoulder level and 'Papa' when their left hands were moved in the same way, and Maelzel took out a patent for his invention in 1834. An advertisement of the time says: 'Pour six francs je remue les yeux et je tourne la tête. Pour dix francs, je dis Papa et Maman.'

The firm of Bru, doll makers, seem to have had a special interest in mechanical things, and in 1869 Monsieur Bru took out a patent for perfecting the manufacture of dolls, having made a doll in 1867, which turned its head showing two expressions. It was in 1887 or the following year that Thomas Edison, inventor of the phonograph, turned his attention to the problems of the speaking doll and adapted a phonograph with round discs to go inside a doll. The result was a talking doll, whose remarks could be varied by merely changing the disc, like changing the record on the gramophone. These dolls were shown first at the Paris Exhibition, and then at the Lennox Lyceum, New York City, and were described as follows: 'Twelve daintily dressed phonograph dolls standing in a row on a miniature theatre stage delighted fathers and mothers by repeating each in turn a verse from our well beloved *Mother Goose*. The voices were high pitched and taken together rather monotonous. But the pleasure of a child who has one of these dolls promises to be endless, if he or she can restrain the instinct to find out where the voice comes from, for the firm who sells them will soon be able to put in the new phonograms with fresh verses, whenever the little owner desires it.'

The *Société Française de Fabrication des Bébés et Jouets* also made a phonograph doll for the Paris Exhibition of 1900, but it was not manufactured after the Exhibition, as although mechanically ingenious, it cost far too much to produce in any large quantities. For the same reason no doubt, there is only one Edison phonograph doll which is known to exist; it belongs to the Thomas Alva Edison Foundation in New Jersey. The phonograph was not the only method used to make dolls 'speak'; one talking and crying doll of the 1880s was operated by blowing sharply down a tube.

Nowadays the child is offered a vast number of speaking dolls, such as 'Chatty Cathy', who can say fifteen phrases from 'I love you' to 'It's my birthday'. Walking dolls and a fantastic series of battery operated toys from Hong Kong and Japan are also a commonplace of the modern nursery. As one contemplates these – the tin pig frying the eggs in his pan, and tossing them; the fire engines with the ladders which lift into position; the great liner representing the *Titanic* which plays the tune *Nearer my God to thee*, as its lights flash on and off; the bear which blows bubbles – it is a salutary thought in the present age of electronics and automation, that nearly all these types of movement were in fact enjoyed in the nineteenth, if not the eighteenth century. The battery toy is cheap and effective, and today every child, not only the children of the rich, can therefore enjoy a movable toy. But, cost apart, the children of the last century could enjoy walking toys and speaking toys very similar to those we have today.

Perhaps as electronics and automation develop, some fascinating new movements will be added to playthings. But one doubts whether the elegance and decorative quality of the automata of the eighteenth century will be surpassed.

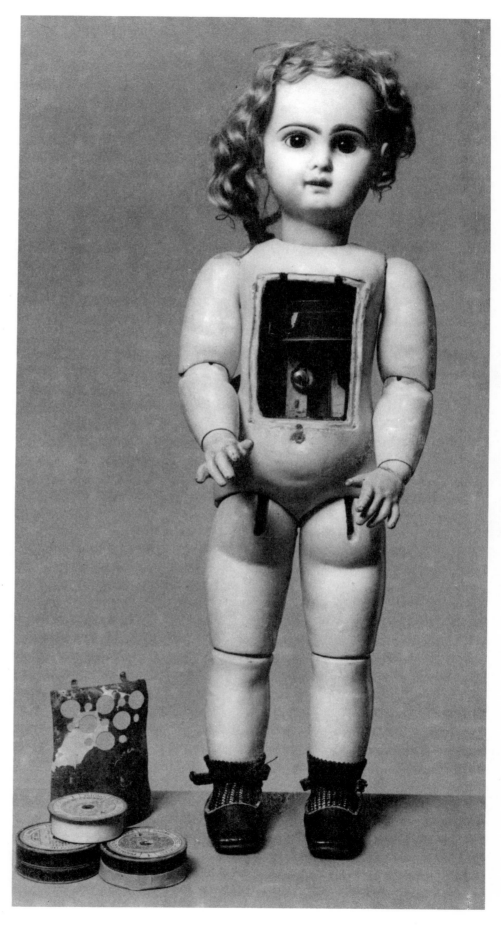

144 *A Jumeau doll of about 1880 with a built-in gramophone turn-table and three changeable discs*

8 Optical Toys and the Juvenile Theatre

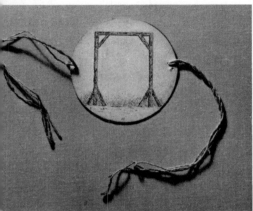

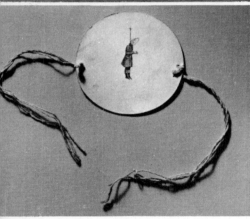

145 Two sides of an example of the Thaumotrope designed by John Ayrton Paris, dating from 1825–7. Paris, who was President of the Royal College of Physicians, used this Thaumotrope to demonstrate the persistence of vision. By twisting the strings the figures on each of its sides are presented with such quick transition that they both appear at the same instant; thus the malefactor is seen hanging from the gibbet. These 'optical toys' represent the earliest known illustrations of the fundamental principle upon which cinematography is based

146 Opposite Madame Danton, wife of Georges Jacques Danton, 1759–94, with an instrument called an Optique

In the nineteenth century the life of the plaything becomes more closely linked with the life of the child. This century sees the development of the educational toy and a corresponding trend towards books which combine instruction with pleasure. It is not surprising that the era which produced a man like Prince Albert, consort of Queen Victoria, should also produce a spate of educational toys. The 1851 Exhibition, which was the product of his spirit, had an enormous educational section. The toys which the Prince Consort approved for his children were eminently sensible, where they were not strictly educational – for example the miniature gardening tools and wheelbarrow (figure 185), to enable the young princes and princesses to pull their weight in tending the garden at Osborne. Maria Edgeworth, whose views on toys have been quoted earlier, but who belongs in time to this section, would have thoroughly approved of the Prince Consort, for she named the rake and wheelbarrow among suitable toys to be given to children, as well as a carpenter's bench, and equipment to encourage cooking and chemistry – both described as 'excellent arts if well taught' – and cheap microscopes to encourage an interest in mineralogy.

All this is a novel development in the sphere of playthings. With the optical toys of the nineteenth century especially, one discerns a new didactic spirit in the art of the toymaker. These have a special interest for us today, when some contemporary artists are showing a preoccupation with the intricacies of optics. The 1965 Exhibition of Optical Art at the Museum of Modern Art, New York, contained a number of exhibits which could as well have fitted into an exhibition of English Victorian optical toys as into the current Op Art movement.

The Thaumatrope, possibly the earliest among these, was invented in 1825 by Dr John Ayrton Paris, not Sir John Herschel as is sometimes claimed. The Thaumatrope consisted of paper discs with different images on each side, which if rotated fast, flowed together, with the result that a parrot was seen to go into a cage, a bald man to put on his wig (figure 145). It was the custom for parents to buy a box full of 'thaumatropical amusement'.

The Phenakisticope (figure 151), was invented in 1833 by Plateau of Ghent, and was in fact exactly the same as the Strotoscope invented at the same moment by Stampfer of Vienna. Both of these worked on the principle of rotating cogs and wheels, and the English toy equivalent is variously called Tantascope, Phantascope, Phantamascope, Magic Disc or Kaleidorama – so many names for the same toy merely go to show the great interest in toys of this kind. A great many of them were issued by the Holborn firm of Clarke, which was also known for selling all aspects of Juvenile Drama.

The Zoetrope (figure 155), was first invented in principle as the Daedalum or Wheel of Life by W.H.Horn of Bristol in 1832, but it was first patented by a Frenchman in 1860 and not marketed as a Zoetrope before 1867 in England. The same contrivance was brought out in America, also in 1867, by Milton Bradley.

It consisted of a metal drum, capable of revolving easily, which was pierced by a series of thin slots and then pivoted on a heavy base, on its axis. It was accompanied by a series of paper strips giving figures in various stages of movement, and as it rotated the figures appeared to move by 'persistence of vision'.

Milton Bradley, born in Maine in 1836, produced numbers of games and home amusements during his long career. He was an excellent business man, and when the Zoetrope had been on sale in America about ten years, he leased rights for its use to the Ray and Taylor Manufacturing Company of Springfield, who made men's haberdashery. The firm put out a 'Zoetrope collar box' containing ten of the latest style men's collars and three sets of pictures for the Zoetrope – which the box became when the collars were removed. The price for the whole lot, collars, box and pictures was twenty cents.

The Zoetrope reflected the nineteenth-century preoccupation with movement and light, which was to lead eventually to the invention of the camera. In 1878 when Edward Muybridge made his epoch-making experiments towards the development of cinematography, with separate pictures of a horse cantering, he used a Zoetrope to analyse the progress of the horse's movements. There is clearly a strong connection between certain toys and the cinema. Mr Stanley Donen, the film director, who has made a collection of toys of movement, tells me he is convinced that his interest in mechanical toys as a child led on to his interest in the cinema.

Later developments in optics tie in with developments in the juvenile theatre. The Praxinoscope, for example, was developed as being less glaring to the eye than the earlier Phenakistiscope and Zoetrope. This mechanism was based on two drums, where the figures were in full movement and the scenery remained still, and the Praxinoscope Theatre based on the same principles enjoyed great popularity. The Tachyscope, invented by F. Reynaud in 1877 used the same principle as the Zoetrope, but instead of hand-drawn pictures, photographs taken by a still camera are used.

The Chromatrope worked by the use of torsion applied to coloured discs; by flicking them quickly, the watcher gets the illusion of movement, so that moving geometrical patterns in colour are projected to coalesce and dissolve, and give the effect of a self-operating kaleidoscope. Later 'New Chromotrope' slides were made, hand-operated on the cog-wheel principle. These were beautiful and also wide in range: a parent bird flies to feed its nestlings, and disappears from sight as the other parent approaches from the opposite direction; a ship heaves on a billowing wave; a butterfly flutters around a garden; a windmill turns its sails. The Kaleidoscope, which is still immensely popular today, began as a toy for adults, before it was taken over by children.

But, of course, the real advance towards the age of cinematography lay in the sphere of the Magic Lantern (figure 161), and the effective advance in the projection of pictures, static or moving, was from the stage when a single viewer looked through a peephole, slot or eye-glass, to that of audience viewing. Early versions of the Magic Lantern were in fact toys, not grown-up experiments. Selina Trimmer is said to have used it in order to instruct the children of the Duchess of Devonshire in the eighteenth century. Early versions of it were produced in numbers in England, France and America by 1840; they were made of bronzed tin and were extremely ornamental, selling for about 7s 6d each. Hand-painted coloured slides would be used. From here it was a short step to the invention of all sorts of moving slides – slipping slides, lever action slides, rack slides and 'New Chromotrope' slides.

147 A Praxinoscope Theatre made in France by Emile Reynaud in 1878. The scenery on the lid of the box remains still while the drum containing the figured slides is revolved. Both are reflected in a mirror, the figures appearing animated against a static background

The American Polyopticon, and the French Panoptique, two further types of
Magic Lantern, both represented the nineteenth-century fascination with photography in its early forms. The Panoptique used home-made pictures out of maga-
zines, and, in a typical nineteenth-century fashion, many had highly moral captions;
pictures from Bunyan's *Pilgrim's Progress* were a characteristic series used. The
Polyopticon was a cheaper version of the Magic Lantern; but actual Magic Lanterns
were also imported from Europe to the United States, although the better ones
were distinctly expensive, and thus limited to the richer households. In 1819
W. B. Gilley advertised in *The New York Commercial Advertiser* that he had for
sale a 'Magic Lantern – 96 glasses – upwards of 250 subjects – Ancient and Modern
History from the creation to 1806' – and we note once again the instructive subject
matter so typical of the time.

By the end of the century, the Americans were beginning to make their own
contribution to the need for toys which satisfied the curiosity aroused by photography and the early cinema. Longer versions of the old Zoetrope were produced.
One of these was called the Kittiscope, put on sale by Selchow and Righter in 1908
and advertised as an 'American made moving picture machine'. There were now
stereopticons for viewing double postcards specially printed for the purpose, and
other projectors for enlarging coloured cards on the screen. But obviously the
German hold on the magic lantern business was still extremely formidable, for
Buckeye Stereopticon Company of Cleveland felt impelled to make an anguished
appeal to the trade: 'Don't handle imported magic lanterns – we have them skinned'.

There were many different types of optical amusements throughout the nineteenth century. The catalogue of an exhibition held in 1956 by the Moving Picture
Museum Association mentions a rare one: the so-called New Optical Amusement
of 1890 which demonstrates another means of obtaining movement by means of
slides. It consists of a wooden box with a sliding lid, 10 in. by 2 in. by 2 in., and
several hand painted glass slides, with such subjects as flying-birds, a sailing ship,
or a galloping horse. When inserted into the back of the box, in front of an aperture,
the eye-piece is rotated with the use of a well-cut, multi-faceted piece of glass, and
the spectator can see several copies of the same image dissolving into a moving
picture.

The dividing line between the optical toy and the peep-show is often hard to
draw. There is the same emphasis on instruction and subjects likely to improve or
broaden the mind, while in the method in which they are displayed there is the
same adventurous preoccupation with new methods with which to attract the
public.

Actual panoramas were invented in 1785 by Robert Barker, an Edinburgh
painter. The audience sat in the middle while a continuous moving picture of an
entire area was pulled past them and around them. Small toy panoramas were
thereafter published by many print-sellers including Spooner, Reeves & Sons and

Mr. T.P. Cooke, as Ben. Treenant.

Mr. N.T. Hicks, as Ned. Martin.

No 2 Mr. R. Honner, as Jan Dousterswyvel.

Mrs. R. Honner, as Rose Linden.

Jersey. Pubd by G. SKELT, 24, Clearview St. Saint Helier.

151 Opposite *Phenakisticope discs invented and patented by the Belgian, Plateau, in 1832. The viewer stood in front of a mirror and looked at the reflection of the disc through the slots, while spinning the bone handle. The figures appear to be moving, demonstrating persistence of vision*

Ackermann in London; these toy panoramas, which consisted of a pictorial strip to be gradually unrolled from a cylindrical box, might be feet, or yards long; they were not however comparable in splendour to the public panoramas.

In 1868 Bradley, whose name has been mentioned in connection with the Zoetrope, manufactured the 'Historoscope – Panorama and History of America from Columbus to the Civil War'. This was a box with one side cut out as if to show the stage of a theatre. Into the opening came a series of panoramic pictures in colour, illustrating the highlights of American history, the pictures being printed on a long strip of paper which wound round two rollers within the box. A similar but smaller device was the 'Myriopticon' showing a historical panorama of the Civil War.

The panoramas were succeeded in popularity by the dioramas. These employed the method of revolving the audience, instead of revolving the pictures. Toy dioramas, measuring 6 ins by $7\frac{1}{2}$ ins were made inside a cardboard frame: they were transparencies to be viewed by reflected and transmitted light. A typical subject of dioramas and panoramas in miniature was the Funeral of the Duke of Wellington of which there is a good example by Henry Alken in the R. J. Abbey Collection. Also in the same collection is a view of Naples by George Sala which shows the contemporary preoccupation with scenic beauty and geography.

Yet another form of animated home peep-show into which three people could look at the same time, was the Kinora. This was a smaller and more compact version of the public Mutascope, which presented an animated picture of good quality and reasonable duration. The Kinora was especially suitable for home use because it had easily replaceable reels.

The Great Exhibition of 1851 provided another favourite nineteenth-century peep-show subject, as did the opening of the Thames Tunnel. There is a good example by Heinrich Keller, in the R. J. Abbey Collection. Even eggs were pressed into use as a form of peep-show in the nineteenth century. We have seen how from the earliest times the egg shape is a formative toy shape, and in the nineteenth century it takes an instructional form in the use of so-called peep-eggs. For some deep psychological reason, collectors have always been fascinated by eggs, whether alabaster, painted china, or even richly jewelled as in Russian Fabergé objects. Each peep-egg, which was made of alabaster, contained two scenes, which were viewed through a double convex lens, inserted in the top of the body. Favourite subjects for them, popular also for panoramas, were the Clifton Suspension Bridge and Nightingale Valley, as well as the Noah's Ark, which was presumably favoured also for its religious connections.

150 One of the original illustrations to R. L. Stevenson's essay on the Juvenile Theatre: Penny Plain and Twopence Coloured *published in 1884*

Akin to peep-eggs was a process invented by the London Stereoscopic Company by which an outline of an object in metal was set in a vertical metal spindle, so that when it revolved the complete object was seen. This same toy had in fact appeared earlier in France under the title of 'la toupie éblouissante'.

The Juvenile Theatre, quite apart from more static versions like panoramas, reached the zenith of its popularity in the first forty years of the nineteenth century. Obviously many elements contributed to the popularity of the Juvenile Theatre – the natural love of all children for the dramatic and not least dressing-up. There is an attractive nineteenth-century lithograph after Aubry called *Les Petits Acteurs* which seems to sum up the child's love of costume: one child pulls on long boots, another buttons a waistcoat over a cushion, while yet another poses haughtily in a cocked hat in the background. Since the days of the Greeks children have enjoyed dressing-up, and obviously the arrival of the Juvenile Theatre did something to

Grindoff

"THE VILLAIN'S SCOWL."

152 *A vignetted plate of the characters in* Harlequin Robin Hood, *published in 1843 by J. K. Green*

153 *An illustration of* Beauty and the Beast *as performed at the Royal Coberg Theatre, 1820. This sheet was published by West and the story shown here is of the usual melodramatic character*

154 *A sheet from the Juvenile Theatre showing Skelt's* New Fairies

gratify this urge, quite apart from the more homely method of wearing their parents' clothes.

Was the rise of the Juvenile Theatre also connected with the adult passion for drama? A.E. Wilson believes that this drama-in-miniature was always in the nature of a plaything, for the reason that it was always known by the name of Juvenile Theatre. He traces the first plays, dated 1811, back to the German Toy Theatre plays of the late eighteenth century, when the Augsburg engravers were at work on sheets which he believes to bear striking likenesses to the English 'penny plain, twopence coloured' sheets which were available before the close of the century. Toy model theatres were also made in Vienna in the late eighteenth century, which ties in with this theory.

However, George Speaight, in his work on the history of the English toy theatre entitled *Juvenile Drama* discounts the Wilson theory. He traces the English sheets back to theatrical portraits of the eighteenth century, full length coloured portraits of actors and actresses in their favourite roles, which about the year 1810 developed into four small theatrical portraits on one sheet, instead of one large one. According to Speaight's theory, to give the sheets a common interest all four actors or actresses would be dressed as characters from the same play. The sheet would be headed 'Characters in such-and-such a play as performed at such-and-such a Theatre' and beneath each figure would be written the name of the actor and the part he was playing. But soon it became obvious that to provide an adequate souvenir of a play, more than four characters would have to be represented. The next stage was to print six slightly smaller characters on a sheet and issue two or more sheets for each play, as in two sheets published in 1811: 'Principal Characters in the Popular Pantomime of *The Fairy of the Oak or Harlequin's Regatta. As performed with unbounded applause at Astley's Amphitheatre*'. The next stage, in Speaight's view, was to pass from a few characters to all the characters, in fact an entire reproduction of the play, for if the characters, why not the scenes? The

155 Some Zoetrope discs and strips. The Zoetrope was first invented by W.H. Horn of Bristol in 1832 and patented in America in 1867 by Milton Bradley. It consists of a metal drum which pivots on a heavy base, on its axis. The drum is pierced by a succession of long narrow slots and inside are placed paper strips illustrated with figures in various stages of movement; on rotating the drum the figures became animated. The Zoetrope contributed to the invention of the camera and was an important step in the development of cinematography

156 Les Metamorphoses *or polyoptic pictures, printed for Jullien by Walter Frère in Paris about 1850. These polyoptic pictures are distorted in such a manner that when a highly polished speculum is placed in the circle indicated on the card, the reflection is found to be normal and free from distortion*

only thing now lacking was the Book of Words, and in due course this too appeared. So Juvenile Drama was born.

George Speaight's view is convincing (although there seems no reason why the German sheets should not also have influenced the Regency ones for a number of different elements could have gone into the making of Juvenile Drama). Surely, however, it is correct to suppose that Juvenile Theatre grew directly out of adult theatre – for the exactness of the finish of the toy sheets, the exquisite details of the early drawings indicate that they were not originally conceived as playthings, which would surely have been given a rougher, more impressionistic, less detailed treatment.

In fact the Juvenile Theatre sprang from the early nineteenth-century passion for the theatre, containing within it many different elements, that created a new fashion which took the Regency nursery by storm. The methods used to make the actual sheets were extremely painstaking. The script would come from a condensed version of the actual play; it was also sometimes written down from memory, and where necessary bowdlerised. The artists would visit the theatres to make notes for the scenery and costumes. The characters, as can be seen in the illustrations (figures 149 and 150) were always shown in their most striking attitudes – striking attitudes thus becoming one of the hallmarks of Juvenile Drama. The drawings were engraved and the scenes were subsequently sold in two sizes: $8\frac{1}{2}$ ins $\times$ $6\frac{1}{2}$ ins or 12 ins $\times$ $9\frac{1}{4}$ ins.

This engraving was a slow process, but produced none-the-less delightful results. Four basic colours were used – gamboge, prussian blue, carmine and black, but these were combined to make other colours. However, aesthetically one tends to prefer the black and white or 'penny plain' variety to the 'twopence coloured'.

The great collection of sheets assembled by the London lawyer Ralph Thomas, based on the earlier Hodges collection, and now lying in the Prints and Drawings room of the British Museum, shows a highly attractive and imaginative level of art (figures 152 and 153). The earliest sheets in the British Museum are published by J.K. Green, although as we have seen sheets were known in Germany before this. Green was therefore probably just ahead in time of William West or R. Lloyd. Eminent artists who worked in this field included George and Isaac Cruikshank, Flaxman, Dighton, Finden and even according to some optimistic legends William Blake himself. Artists were paid £2 for each plate of original drawings approved.

The plays all have highly melodramatic titles, and merely to read a list of them gives an indication of the histrionic level of this form of entertainment: *Beauty and the Beast* (figure 153); *Blue Beard*; *The Brave Cossack*; *Black-eyed Susan*; *The Grand Melodrama of the Broken Sword*; *The Brigand*; *The Casket of Gloriana* (a Grand Eastern Melodrama which includes a typical Juvenile Drama character called Rimbozzi the Black Enchanter). All these titles were published by West between 1815 and 1825. The Harlequin series was always popular with children (figure 152), and of the many tales in the Harlequin series, Harlequin Whittington was probably drawn by George Cruikshank. *Bertram* and *Guy Mannering*, published by West, are two series which have been attributed to the pen of William Blake, on the evidence of the W.B. monogram. Despite the excellence of the work, there seems absolutely no proof that the great artist was, in fact, responsible for them, so one must reluctantly abandon this legend of the toy theatre, taking comfort in the verdict of George Speaight: 'This popular cheap form of what is essentially a folk art does not need the attraction of the names of famous artists to advertise its

157 An illustration from Williamson's The European in India, *1813, showing a group of people watching a toy theatre*

158 A toy theatre of about 1800, with small dressed dolls belonging to it. Now in the Victoria and Albert Museum, this theatre is believed to have originally been used in a school for young ladies

*159 A lever slide for a Magic Lantern.
By working the lever up and down the
skipping rope appears to turn and the girl
to jump over it. This slide, made in
England, has been signed and dated
M 1857*

*161 Opposite A French Lampascope or
Magic Lantern for use with an ordinary
domestic paraffin table lamp. Made in
about 1870*

*160 The slide projected in the Praxino-
scope theatre on page 125*

wares. It was born in the gutter, and though for a time it flaunted itself in quite high company, the anonymity of the gutter is its true resting place.'

Perhaps the word 'gutter' is placing the toy theatre a little low, for although its popularity certainly declined after the thirties Juvenile Drama has a rich and interesting history throughout the rest of the century. In 1830, the height of its popularity, there were thirty publishers in the business in London. Of these the best known were Matthew Skelt, West, Green and Webb, with Pollock coming on the scene later.

Skelt has been blamed for the decline in quality of the toy sheets as the century progressed, after 1840; but although it is true that he sold some sheets for a half-penny, instead of a penny, so did both Green and West. R. L. Stevenson, in his poetic article on the whole enchanted world of Juvenile Drama, published in 1884, one of the original woodcuts from which is illustrated (figure 150), expresses a special sympathy for Skelt, based it seems on his name, which he prefers to that of Webb – to the detriment of Webb's reputation. Stevenson wrote: 'The name of Skelt has always seemed a part and parcel of the charm of his productions. It may be different with the rose, but the attraction of this paper drama sensibly declined when Webb had crept into the rubric: a poor cuckoo flaunting in Skelt's nest . . . Indeed this name of Skelt appears so stagey and piratic that I will adopt it boldly to design these qualities. Skeltery, then, is a quality of much art.' And Stevenson goes on to describe under the generic name of Skeltery his romantic passion for Juvenile Drama.

Perhaps Skelt was not such a hero as Stevenson makes out, but he was also not such a villain as to be solely responsible for the decline of the popularity of Juvenile Drama. This was due to a variety of causes, firstly the advance of the English stage from the age of melodrama to that of realism. Juvenile drama had thrived on the current fashion for melodrama. The oriental processions, abducted maidens, wicked uncles, spectacular effects, trick changes so popular in pantomimes today, were all especially suited to adaptation to the junior stage. But the junior stage was correspondingly unsuited to subtle delineation of character, literary dialogue and the discussion of ideas, and when these concepts were introduced to the theatre, current productions could no longer be adapted with success, and Juvenile Drama lost much of its immediacy. Ibsen and Shaw were hardly suited to Pollock and West.

Secondly, the advent of the illustrated press fulfilled much the same purpose as the sheets had fulfilled earlier – journals with coloured pictures now filled the long winter evenings, as earlier the sheets had done. Thirdly, the advent of photography finally killed the immediacy of the sheets, even more effectively than the illustrated press. Finally cinema and television provide modern children with an outlet for their natural interest in drama more effectively and quickly than the sheets had ever done.

This is not to say that the toy theatre immediately dwindled and died after the 1840s. On the contrary the toy theatre of the 1870s was enjoyed by such varied characters as Dickens, Ellen Terry, G. K. Chesterton, and Winston Churchill, as well as Stevenson. But perhaps these later devotees felt what modern children feel – that it was more fun to plan the drama and colour the sheets than to actually enact the play. C. B. Cochran expresses very well in his reminiscences the feeling we have all experienced: 'The pleasure of the toy theatre was in anticipation rather than in realization. I don't think I ever got through a performance of an entire play. Certainly the audience never stayed through from beginning to end.' Goethe,

162 A scene from James Flaunty or the Terror of the Western Seas *from the Juvenile Theatre. This was designed by J. B. Yeats, Irish artist and brother of the poet W. B. Yeats, in 1901, when efforts were made to revive this form of folk art*

who had a childhood passion for the toy theatre, laid his finger on another aspect of it when in *Wilhelm Meister* Wilhelm recounts to Marianne his delight in playing with puppets so long as performances were reserved for the fifth acts 'where the cutting and stabbing lay'.

The modern child, presented with the exquisite toy theatres, an exact copy of the nineteenth-century ones, obtainable from Pollock's Toy Museum in London where the tradition is still carried on, probably feels a Goethean desire to perform the fifth violent act, if he does not totally agree with Cochran that the pleasure is anticipation rather than realization. However, the history of Pollock's Toy Museum is an interesting commentary on the way the tradition of Juvenile Drama still continues more than a century after its heyday. Pollock of Hoxton Street and Clarke of Garrick Street continued to sell sheets in the 1870s onwards, as did H. J. Webb, of Old Street. Benjamin Pollock died in 1937, just after his eightieth birthday, having lived and worked at Hoxton Street for sixty years. After his death his two daughters carried on until the shop was blasted by a bomb which fell in Hoxton Street; thereafter, in 1945 an antiquarian bookseller Alan Kean bought up the Miss Pollocks' stock, and formed a company, which, in spite of encouragement from many eminent actors and others interested in the history of the theatre, eventually ended, owing to the difficulties of making a commercial success of this type of business in the straitened circumstances of the immediate post-war years. Mrs. Fawdry, the present owner and manager of Pollock's Toy Museum, then bought up the stock, because her son and his friends wanted more plays for their toy theatres, and found herself eventually founding the present charming monument to childhood and the toy theatre – Pollock's Toy Museum.

The later attempts to revive the toy theatre in the contemporary idiom did not meet with great success. The sheets shown here (figure 162) by the Irish painter

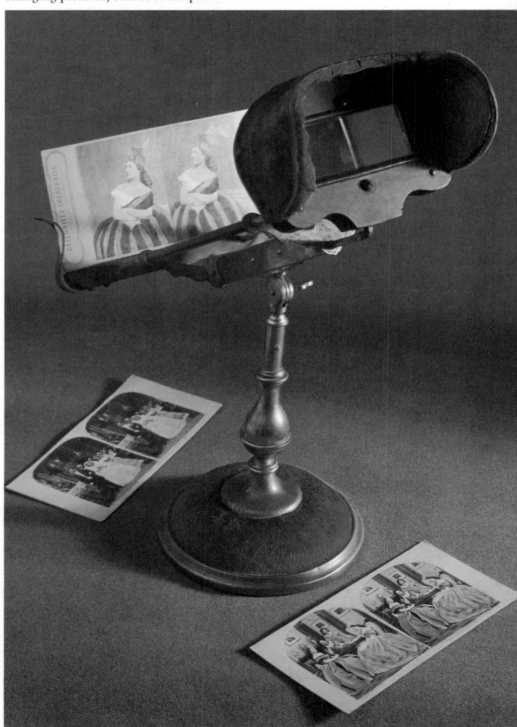

164 Opposite *An intricate toy theatre; a copy of the original copper-plate engraving commissioned by John Reddington in 1845–50. The printed sheets are cut out and stuck on to wood to make a theatre and figures can be bought for a number of plays including* Dick Turpin *and* Aladdin

Jack B. Yeats, brother of the Irish poet, represent an attempt in the 1900s to revive it as a form of folk art. 'James Flaunty or the Terror of the Western Seas' was published in 1901, and two more in 1902 and 1903. The scenes were printed in book form with accompanying text, and although highly attractive and vivid, like all the art of Jack B. Yeats, one is at liberty to doubt whether they were really used in a very practical way. Nowadays the colourful original plays produced by Pollock's Toy Museum are really a better memorial to the history of Juvenile Drama for the average child, because they provide in Stevenson's words: 'Kaleidoscopes of changing pictures, echoes of the past'.

163 A Victorian pedestal Stereoscope, chromium finished with red plush covering on base and lenshood. The Stereoscope, patented and made in 1885, gives a 3-D effect to a picture

9 More Nineteenth-Century Toys

The nineteenth century was marked by a rapid development in the number and variety of toys, which spread far beyond those toys which can strictly be described as educational. In the next chapter the whole vivid world of nineteenth-century dolls and their accoutrements will be considered – here I wish to outline the enormous variety of toys which were available to the child of this period, whatever its country.

A typical nineteenth-century plaything was the puppet (figure 165). Puppets have a historical unity, which makes them especially attractive. Even today the puppet shows of Sicily continue to enact legends of the rescue of Clorinda by Tancred and the victories of the Christians over the infidels – centuries after the crusades have been forgotten by the grown-up world. Puppets were known to the Greeks and Romans and also to the Chinese, and if string puppets are basically outside the scope of a work on children's toys, they cannot be omitted altogether from a catalogue of nineteenth-century toys, because of the enormous popularity of glove puppets at this time.

In nineteenth-century France traditional fairy tales and humorous subjects were also presented by the shadow theatre – Père Endel is known to have given a show at Crotoy in France; it was customary to give a Punch and Judy show in the day, and a shadow show in the evening. The origins of the shadow theatre are indeed extremely ancient and stretch back a long way beyond the nineteenth century; the Chinese had known and developed the art with great success. The Wayang culture of Java makes great use of shadow puppets (figure 169) and has done so from early times.

165 The French puppet theatre is illustrated in the engraving 'Les Petites Marionnettes' from Le Bon Genre, published in France in 1820

166 *An illustration of the ever-popular* Punch *and* Judy *performing to an audience, from* Punch *or* May Day *by* B. R. Haydon

167 Left *Nineteenth-century American jack-in-the-boxes. The origins of this toy are not known but its former name of 'Punch-Box' may be significant as the faces of the Jacks are often similar to that of Punch*

169 *An early nineteenth-century Javanese shadow puppet, now in the Raffles Collection in the British Museum*

168 Bottom left *An ornate bugle which belonged to the King of Rome, son of Napoleon*

The art of the Wayang stage in present day Indonesia divides itself into three groups: firstly the Purwa group, which holds on firmly to the ancient stories of ancient kings; secondly the Suluh group, which according to a modern Indonesian pamphlet has 'strict enlightenment quality, and new decorative-naturalistic puppets made in atmosphere of western intellectualism'; and thirdly the Pantja-Sila group 'of strongly educational character wanting to apply the five principles of the young Republic as its leitmotif for a remodelling of the old cultural heritage'. The pamphlet however admits that of the three the ancient Wayang Purwa is by far the most popular, and this is played with leather silhouettes, beautifully painted, of such a form that they cast a shadow against a white screen, in order to tell ancient mythical tales. This type of shadow theatre was not confined to the Javanese, but was also known to the Balinese.

Whereas the Chinese puppets were for entertainment, the Javanese were religious in purpose, and the theatres so arranged that the men saw the figures and the women and children saw only shadows. The principal characters of the Javanese Wayang Purwa were princes, princesses, and animals as well as grotesque figures, whereas the principal figures of the Pekin theatre were peasants, students, demons, wicked counsellors, clowns and servants. There is an excellent collection of Javanese shadow puppets in the British Museum, made by Sir Stamford Raffles.

The shadow show was not confined to the Far East, but spread to Turkey, probably via Persia, where its chief character was a slapstick character known as Karagoz. He is mentioned as early as the seventeenth century in the journal of the traveller Thevenot; his name meant Black-eye and it is believed it originally lampooned a statesman called Quaraquisch. Certainly this stock character tends to appear in every puppet play rather as Punch does, and he probably shares an ancestry with Punch, as both are descended from the antique Circurricus, and the Neapolitan Pulcinella.

Still later, the shadow theatre was taken over by the Greek National Theatre (curiously perhaps in view of the present antipathy of Greeks and Turks) and even today shadow plays are used as curtain-raisers to plays on themes of independence.

The nineteenth century certainly saw an increase in the popularity of puppets,

170 A dolls' house, style about 1860, made by Thomas Risley in 1889. The house is of carved and painted wood with conservatory and coach house attached

quite apart from the shadow theatre. Victorian England witnessed the success of the glove puppet, often in the shape of a monkey, and the enormous influence of the Punch and Judy show in the lives of children. John Ruskin tells a curious story of the part which Punch and Judy played in his own sad crabbed childhood: 'The law was that I should find my own amusement. No toys of any kind were at first allowed – and the pity of my Croydon aunt for my monastic poverty in this respect was boundless. On one of my birthdays thinking to overcome my mother's resolution by splendour of temptation, she bought the most radiant Punch and Judy she could find in all the Soho Bazaar – as big as a real Punch and Judy, all dressed in scarlet and gold, and that would dance tied to the leg of a chair. I must have been greatly impressed, for I remember well the look of the two figures, as my aunt exhibited their virtues. My mother was obliged to accept them, but afterwards told me it was not right I should have them. I never saw them again.' Other Victorian children were more fortunate than John Ruskin and enjoyed to the full the barbaric gaiety of the Punch and Judy show.

In nineteenth-century Germany the marionette theatre was taken extremely seriously. Professional authors actually wrote for it, although previously items in the repertoire had been handed down orally. The puppet theatre of Geisselbrecht, a Viennese by origin, who travelled all over Germany, was considered the finest in Germany in the first quarter of the century. Both Ulm and Cologne at the same time had their own marionette theatres, which made use of local situations and dialects with success, while in Hamburg the hand-puppet theatre flourished in the middle of the nineteenth century and owed much to the actor Kuper, who skilfully gave his puppets characteristic local touches. Where local inspiration failed, there were always the stock pieces of the puppet theatre; however a list of their titles makes one doubt whether these puppets were strictly toys, and were not merely occasionally enjoyed by children, in company with the adults for whom they were intended. The titles are certainly highly melodramatic, including such lurid ones as *The King of the Alps and the Enemy of Man*; *The Death Bell at Midnight*; *The London Body Snatchers*; *The Murder in the Wine Cellar* and *The Devils Mill on the Viennese Hills*.

In Italy the marionette theatre held a position not far in importance from that of the professional stage; even grand opera was known to have been produced in an Italian marionette theatre. Characteristically the Spanish puppet theatre had a half-romantic half-religious repertoire and when *The Death of Seneca* was presented at Valencia in 1808 the blood flowed in streams (by means of red ribbons) while at the close the heathen philosopher went to heaven and made a profession of faith.

The French puppet theatre was altogether more sophisticated, as well as extremely popular. Among its devotees was the novelist Georges Sand, who established a complete puppet theatre in her château at Nohant in 1847, whose history is related in *Dernières Pages*. By 1872 120 plays had been presented at this theatre, involving the use of 125 puppets all clothed by Georges Sand. Dialogue was generally improvised (how one would like to have heard it!). Presumably in her puppets she found a solace from the exigencies of her personal life, unlike Thackeray, who was driven to exclaim allegorically in *Vanity Fair*: 'Ah Vanitas, Vanitatum! Which of us is happy in this world? Which of us has his desire? Or having it is satisfied? – Come, children, let us shut up the box and the puppets, for our play is played out.' Georges Sand saw puppets in a kindlier light.

So far we have considered the shadow theatre of the orient, which undoubtedly had a great influence on the puppet theatres of the west, and the popular nineteenth-

171 A wooden pedlar doll selling her wares

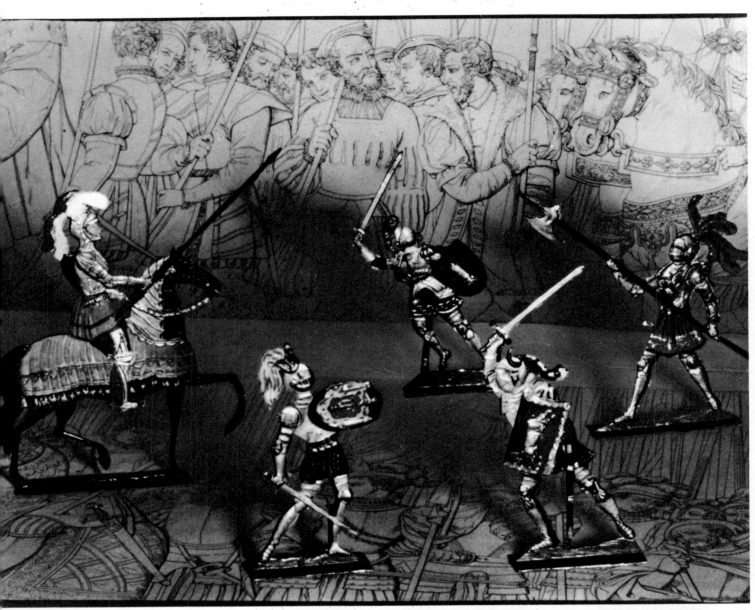

172 Toy soldiers – 'flats' – from the
collection of John G. Garratt, made in
Fürth, Germany, about 1830. The
footsoldiers are 4 inches tall

173 Spanish 'flats' dated about 1820

century version of it. But there were other toys in the nineteenth century, neither educational nor semi-adult in their entertainment value, which expressed the spirit of the age. This was a period when soldiers were extremely popular; not perhaps in the flamboyant way of the soldiers of the eighteenth century when the arts of war were given such prominence by Frederick the Great, but in a more universal and widespread manner. One is reminded of Walter Bagehot's sentiments on real life soldiers: 'The soldier . . . of today is not a romantic animal, dashing at forlorn hopes, animated by frantic sentiment, full of fancies as to a lady love or a sovereign; but a quiet grave man . . . despite all manner of *éclat* and eloquence: perhaps, like Count Moltke, "silent in seven languages".' Certainly, the toy soldiers of the nineteenth century should have been able to be silent in seven languages, or almost as many, for it is during this period that they begin to be widely manufactured.

In Germany Hilpert's early pre-eminence was overtaken by Heinrichsen, who started his business in 1839 and won a gold medal for his engraving three years later. In 1848, in an effort to establish some sort of conformity to help collectors in their armies, Heinrichsen established the so-called Nuremberg scale of one and a third inch for a grown man, although not all manufacturers fell into line with it. The Heinrichsen family continued their efforts throughout the century, and after the First World War Heinrichsen III was making such modern types as gas-masked figures. The firm is believed to have finally stopped manufacture in 1945, although, according to Henry Harris, the widow of the last Heinrichsen still makes a few figures for favoured customers.

Returning to the nineteenth century, the German contemporaries of the Heinrichsen family were names such as Allgeyer of Fürth, Denecke of Brunswick, Weygand of Göttingen and Haffner of Fürth (figure 172). The introduction of the Nuremberg scale was an effort to make life easier for the collector: thus the enormous importance of the toy soldier as an item for the collector was now beginning to match its importance as a child's toy. In previous centuries, although grown men might have collected soldiers, they were still toys as opposed to models. The model soldier of the collector, however, can scarcely be considered a toy, but belongs to that hinterland discussed in the first chapter, where the toy meets the collector's passion, and adult fantasy merges with the fantasy of childhood.

In Berlin at the same period Haselbach and Söhlke made wide ranges of popular models for many years, and in Hanover Riecke produced a wide and interesting series of figures. Certainly the manufacturing of soldiers spread over the whole of Germany and Switzerland. In Aarau, the centre of it, the importance lay in the founders Wilhelm Gottschalk and Johann Rudolf Wehrli. The method of making was as follows: the negative forms for both sides were cut out in slate and engraved; they were then laid on each other and the cavity filled with lead. When the figures were set the painting was then done by home-workers. These little figures to some extent rivalled German wooden toys in popularity.

In England at the same period peasant wooden soldiers became the vogue, although not for very long, and apart from a few examples imported later from Sweden and Denmark the fashion died. There were also some plaster soldiers, larger and more realistic than tin or lead models – one of French manufacture even having a head which rotated in its socket. Nevertheless, the breakability of the material prevented them from ever being enormously popular. The English children were certainly playing with lead soldiers by 1868. Hollow soldiers were first made by William Britain in England by a secret process and in this case it was Germany which copied England and later made hollow soldiers, thus changing her methods of manufacture. Later not only Germany but also Japan pirated English methods in this direction.

Throughout the nineteenth century there are records of soldiers belonging to the children of the famous, showing that as a toy they continued to win hearts, as no doubt they will always do, so long as the martial spirit arises in the child's breast. The King of Rome, son of Napoleon, had gold soldiers, the work of J.B.Claude Oliot, the Emperor's goldsmith. One hundred and seventeen pieces, of the 22nd Light Artillery, the traditional regiment of Corsica, were given to the King by his parents in 1812. In 1814 the display was rescued by Napoleon's sister, Queen Hortense, from the débâcle, and by 1822 returned to the little exile, with some alterations on the figures to make them resemble Austrian soldiers. They were returned to the Imperial family at the time of the Second Empire and altered again, in this case the Imperial eagle was restored, and the soldiers were thus considered fit to become the playthings of the Prince Imperial. In 1870 they were given to the de Pierres family by the Empress Eugénie, in whose possession they remain.

Lead soldiers made by Mignot for the Prince Imperial were brought to England by the family when they went into exile; the Empress Eugénie gave some of the soldiers away to collectors, and the remainder to the Duke of Alba. In fact the toy making firm of Mignot still survives in Paris today, having weathered 170 years of soldier-making. Obviously its wares today contain a number of French soldiers, for collectors, but also Greeks, Romans, crusader figures and an interesting range of historical figures including Queen Victoria and Cleopatra.

Heyde of Dresden, mentioned earlier, is one of the best known names for solid figures, and is believed to have begun production 1870. During the seventy years of its existence, the firm's output was prolific and examples were exported all over the world. Their popularity was due to their great variety of postures and types, and the grouping of their assortments in their boxed sets; however, they were not popular in Germany, as collectors there criticised their bad anatomy. Their factory was finally destroyed during the Second World War. The solid figure was certainly slow to evolve and the flat figure virtually dominated the German scene until the 1870s when English influence, and also to a certain extent French influence changed their habits. Haffner and Allgeyer, both of whom exported much to France, led this development. Haffner then dedicated himself to producing solid figures.

Among other materials, papier mâché was used for making soldiers in Germany at the end of the seventeenth century, and twenty years later was also used in France, but the figures were necessarily larger than the normal size of soldier. In the middle of the nineteenth century a sort of compressed card called *carton comprimé* was used in France, and something similar used in Germany up to the Second World War by the firm Elastoholm, which was subsequently bombed.

Soldiers certainly did not fall behind in popularity in the United States. During the war of Independence, war toys naturally rose in popularity, especially at the time that British troops occupied New York City, and as a result the children there were able to have toys imported from abroad. An advertisement in the *Royal Gazette* for December 1777 promises: 'Christmas presents for the young folks who have an affection for the Art Military, consisting of Horse, Foot and Dragoons. Cast in metal, in beautiful uniforms. 18s a dozen.' The nineteenth-century toy company of McLoughlin Brothers, founded probably in 1855, cashed in on the popularity of soldiers in war time, to issue paper soldiers. Paper, cardboard, tin and lead were therefore known to American children in the nineteenth century as the

174 Lead soldiers on parade. Belgian, about 1830

175 A model of a butcher's shop of about 1840. This toy was designed to teach little girls the art of housekeeping

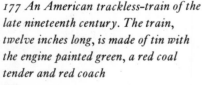

176 The wooden train (above) running down a grooved track was made in about 1845 when many people had never seen a train. The metal one (below) dates from 1873. Both were manufactured in Germany, and the lower one, with 'Stephenson' on it, was clearly for export

material of which their soldiers were made – but these soldiers were imported for the greater part of the century. However, in 1898 C. W. Beiser invented Eureka American soldiers, which took a good deal of the sale away from imported goods. He also invented a cardboard tray in which they could be put away neatly, and fixed without being sewed or stapled down.

Soldiers occupied a great place in the nineteenth-century world of toys, as they did in that of the eighteenth century. But during this period, other new toys also began to appear as interlopers. The toy train for example was an entirely novel sight. In fact commercial production of model trains must clearly have started with the first railways in the 1820s although the history of toy trains precedes that of the invention of the train. Trevithick built a toy steam locomotive before Stephenson constructed the 'Rocket' and brought it up to London to run round Hyde Park for the amusement of the public. Unfortunately his genius was not at the time recognized.

The appeal of trains, unlike the railways themselves, which met with all sorts of obscurantist objections, appears to have been immediate (figure 174). In America in the 1830s and 40s there were several firms producing trackless tin pull locomotives

177 An American trackless-train of the late nineteenth century. The train, twelve inches long, is made of tin with the engine painted green, a red coal tender and red coach

and cars, and such cars were in fact still made into the 1900s, although the greatest era of their popularity was between 1850 and 1890. Early company names were the Merriam Manufacturing Company of Durham, Connecticut, Hull and Stafford of Clinton, Connecticut, and Francis, Field and Francis of Philadelphia. Later came Althof, Bergmann and Co., Leo Schlesinger & Co. of New York and James Fallows & Co. of Philadelphia. Some of these people also made clockwork-powered trackless tin trains: almost all of the trackless tin trains made by the famous firm of Ives were clockwork driven, although in the 1880s they made a few motorless versions of their whistling locomotives.

The first self-propelled tinplate trains made in the United States were brought out in 1856 by George Brown who was active in the clock-making business. Much later a great number of clockwork trains were made by Ives, incorporating such features as working air whistles or cigarette-smoking devices that sent puffs of realistic smoke from the smoke-stack. Such models are naturally much in demand by collectors, as are all genuinely attested Ives locomotives. However, a problem arises in that most of the locomotives made in the 1870s and 80s bear a superficial resemblance to each other, regardless of the manufacturer and there is a danger of some trains being falsely attributed to Ives. Louis H. Hertz, American expert on model trains, thinks that not more than ten or twelve surviving trackless tin clockwork locomotives were made by Ives, since many cheaper models were made by other firms.

Ives, himself, started business in Plymouth, Connecticut, and originally made simple hot-air toys, as well as being a basket maker. He did some of his work at the Blakeslee Carriage Shop in Plymouth and became associated with Blakeslee for some years, to the extent that his first toy company was known as Ives, Blakeslee & Co. Ives then moved to Bridgeport, and bought out the firm of Secor. The combined firm of Ives, Secor was to become one of the most famous in the United States, manufacturing all sorts of mechanical devices both of Ives' own invention, and other people's.

The steam-engine, according to J. T. Van Riekmsdijk of the Science Museum at South Kensington, was hand built in the first fifty years of its life and therefore only within the means of the sons of the rich. The orrery had employed the techniques of clock-making but there was no comparable tradition to be applied

178 A carriage made in silver in Germany at the end of the eighteenth century

179 A cast-iron fire engine steamer made by the Hubley Manufacturing Co., Lancaster, Pa., about 1906

to the making of small boilers and cylinders. Consequently many early pieces are models rather than toys.

By 1870 cheaper models were being made – although they were still made by hand. The models of this date, infinitely pleasing as they are to the eye, are nevertheless not accurate in details. However, the more expensive ones are extremely well made, with many brass castings, and they are elaborately painted. They contain a great deal of brass, copper and steel, but are nevertheless lighter than the real thing. The cheap models at this date, however, were not painted, and took all sorts of liberties with the outline. The characteristics are oscillating cylinders, very tall chimneys and a minimum of four wheels. They have splendid evocative names like Vulcan, Ajax or Hercules.

These earlier steam-driven models captured the essence of the locomotive much more than the later electrically-driven models. Their play value is high, because they demand more attention and skill to get results. Thus we return to our basic thesis that a child really prefers a challenging toy – challenging in the sense that his own skills are needed to make something of it – rather than the perfect toy,

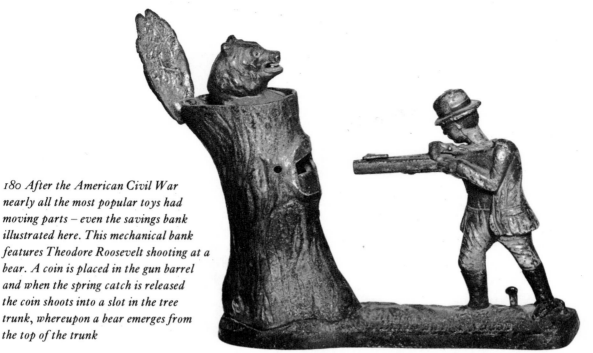

180 After the American Civil War nearly all the most popular toys had moving parts – even the savings bank illustrated here. This mechanical bank features Theodore Roosevelt shooting at a bear. A coin is placed in the gun barrel and when the spring catch is released the coin shoots into a slot in the tree trunk, whereupon a bear emerges from the top of the trunk

whose very perfection can repel or at least bore him.

Although these early steam models were produced mainly in England some also came from France and Germany. In the United States steam trains were manufactured in the 1870s chiefly by Eugene Beggs of Paterson, New Jersey, and continued to be made until the 1900s. Ives also manufactured steam trains of a similar nature. Of course some parents considered steam engines too dangerous for their children, but they were sufficiently popular for Montgomery Ward's catalogue to feature them in 1885. Three engines are mentioned: 'The Hero, for 40 cents, the Ajax at 90 cents (a sensible practical instructive toy) and the Empire at two dollars (warranted to work perfectly, absolutely safe).' There is after all a tremendous natural appeal in a steam engine. Who has not imagined in their time:

> As we rush, as we rush in the train
> The trees and the houses go wheeling back
> But the starry heavens above that plain
> Come flying on our track.

The important toy development of electrical trains could not really make any headway until the dry-cell battery had been invented. In the days when the only known compounds for batteries gave a weak current and lasted only a short time, and when there was no transformer to facilitate the use of household current, an electric train could not possibly be marketed on a large scale. There were a few

181 A painted wooden figure of a horseman and dog, made in Norway between 1850 and 1880

182 Painted wooden dolls, Russian, about 1850. These 'nests' of dolls are still made today, and are extremely popular with children

attempts, and a train that ran was sold in 1896 by Carlisle and Finch; but the era of the electric train falls more properly into the twentieth century, in which geniuses such as Frank Hornby (figure 219), to be considered later in connection with his work with Meccano, did much to stimulate mechanically-minded boys with his inventions.

It was natural for the nineteenth-century inventive genius to turn to trains, away from the automata of the eighteenth century, which were prompted by curiosity about the human body. Certainly in the nineteenth-century interest in trains there must also be something of a power complex, for a steam train is essentially in the power of its creator.

Among other toys popular in the nineteenth century were all sorts of metal toys such as pistols and guns – especially in America after the Civil War. Another American fad was the cast-iron savings bank (figure 180), which was involved in the general trend towards movable toys – nearly all favourite toys at this time have wheels or move somehow, even a savings bank. There are examples of steam boats, as well as the steam trains discussed earlier; even steam mills and steam factories

were produced. Wheel toys with bells were all the rage in the 1860s for children who could ride bicycles, and elaborate bell-ringing toys got more and more elaborate as the century progressed. Steam and electricity were borrowed from the grown-up world to animate a series of toys.

The mechanical banks may perhaps be put into the category of things which are half toys, half fads. Animals often provided inspiration for the banks, as did historical figures. The model shown here of President Roosevelt shooting at a bear combines both tendencies. These mechanical banks have become so prized by collectors that at a sale in New York in the 1950s banks which had gone for one dollar and 4.50 dollars in the days when they were in every shop, then went for 200 or 300 dollars, and even as high as 1200 dollars. In America banks have aroused more of the keen fervour of the collector than any other toy except dolls.

Up till now we have dealt with metal and mechanical toys, but the wooden toy was not forgotten in the nineteenth century, owing to its remarkable and continuing appeal. The Nuremberg toy industry flourished throughout the nineteenth century, making attractive, brightly coloured toys. At the same time at Winchendon in America another Nuremberg was growing up where one firm claimed in 1890 to be the largest wood-toy manufacturer in the world. Despite the Industrial Revolution, the tradition of painstaking craftsmanship continued. Interesting examples of this were the wooden toys carved by British soldiers in Salem, Massachusetts, while they were held prisoner during the American War of Independence. Dolls' cradles and other toys from this source are still in the Essex Institute of Salem.

In England wooden horses had a considerable vogue and the influence of William Morris was felt on plainly carved wooden toys. Morris himself did not actually make any toys, and although it has been suggested that Ernest Gimson, a carpenter who fell under Morris' influence and practised the craft in the Cotswolds, may have made some, I have not been able to find any confirmation of this.

The German wooden toys continued on the same lines as in preceding centuries. The German miniature wooden kitchen made in Nuremberg in particular became extremely popular, and many were exported to France until native products began to be marketed there. Many other characteristic toys of the 'eternal' type, found in every age, enjoyed as much popularity in the nineteenth century as previously, and jostled with steam trains and newcomers like cars.

183 An American nineteenth-century carved wooden ball in a 'cage' with a cone-shaped top
184 Below A wooden horse, painted red, from Hallingdal in Norway. Carved about 1800
185 Below right Typical of his age, Prince Albert thoroughly approved of practical toys. The wheelbarrow and tools were among those made by Brades, Thornhill and others for the use of Queen Victoria's children at Osborne. Each child's initials were painted on his or her barrow (this one was Princess Alice's) and the children received pay for the work they did in the garden and the vegetables they grew there

186 These children's blocks, made in America, are an example of a mid-nineteenth-century educational toy. They are small blocks of various colours, stencilled with the letters of the alphabet, animals, fruit and other objects

187 A constructional toy similar to those made in Germany in the nineteenth century. The set comes with a picture to follow and wooden blocks, arches, windows with inserted glass and doors. Coloured insets as on the clock faces and doors are printed on paper.

188 An illustration of a Victorian nursery: the doll's cradle lies empty on the floor as the little girl shows her mother her doll. From an engraving of 1870

Balls became even more popular when the discovery of rubber gave them a new lease of life as an 'everlasting' toy. Kites can be seen in many nineteenth-century paintings and engravings, enjoyed by children of all classes. Marbles were at the height of their popularity in the 1860s and 70s in England, and sometimes veined glass ones were used, which are now extremely rare. Tops were extremely fashionable in Victorian England, and in the Holt Collection there is a Punching Top with a Boer War motto and a Union Jack. The wooden hoop, an old-established favourite, was joined by the metal hoop driven by the skimmer. The jack-in-the-box (figure 167) a toy whose origins are obscure but whose sixteenth-century name of 'Punch-box' may connect it with the puppet – the faces of the Jacks are often astonishingly similar to that of Punch – is another typical toy of the Victorian child.

Victorian childhood may have been beset by educational theories, but it was also infinitely rich in toys of every variety, from the simple ball, top and kite which had been known for centuries, down to newcomers such as the steam train – a jostling crowd clamouring for the attention of the child fortunate enough to possess them.

189 Two little girls with a doll and a rocking horse, about 1860

10 The Doll and her Belongings

The world of the doll in the nineteenth century is a world of its own. Never have dolls been so prettily enchanting as during this period. Never has so much ingenuity and invention been dedicated to their development, in so many materials, including china, Parian, bisque, rubber, composition and wax, so that some of the nineteenth-century dolls which have survived seem to belong to the same kind of furbelowed and extravagant confections as the large hats of the period.

At the same time dolls are developing and expanding in type as well as material, for this is the age in which the Baby Doll (figure 200), so obvious and beloved a member of the modern child's nursery, first made its appearance. It may seem incredible to us that the baby doll should not have appeared until the 1820s. Early pictures of children with dolls in their arms have all shown them with what are in fact tiny adults (figures 85 and 124). One's mental picture of the seventeenth-century doll is of a tiny, exquisitely and formally dressed object in the arms of its little owner – so like a grown-up that one has to look twice sometimes to see if it is another child or a doll. But then at that time children themselves were dressed as adults, and the cult of childhood itself, so prevalent and so delightful nowadays, did not exist. Children were not only dressed like their parents but expected to behave like them. Nevertheless the absence of the baby doll is still rather curious, considering the natural appeal of the baby to the little girl, and as some of the appeal of any doll must be to the latent mother instinct, surely a baby doll would have appealed even more than one dressed as a grown-up?

Once established, the baby doll enjoyed enormous popularity leading to such splendid examples of the trend as the Eugenic Baby Doll in the United States, described as 'the first doll perfect in mind and body' and the modern baby doll of Mattel Inc. euphoniously named 'Baby Pattaburp' who according to her advertisements: 'Drinks her milk, then burps, after being patted tenderly on the back'.

What was the date of the earliest baby doll? It is true that certain eighteenth-century dolls were apparently intended to represent children, because their dresses have ribbons attached to them at the back, to indicate leading reins. But the real rise of the baby doll was during the nineteenth century, and to argue, as some experts have, that a doll in grown-up clothes may in fact be a baby doll because babies wore grown-up clothes at this period, seems to be begging the question.

In England the first baby doll known was in about 1825, but its true success was intimately connected with that of one of the most famous English firms of dollmakers, namely the family of Montanari. For it was at the Crystal Palace Exhibition of 1851 that the Montanaris were especially noted for the range of their dolls 'from infancy to womanhood' in the words of Tallis' *History and Description of the Crystal Palace Exhibition of the World's Industry in 1851.*

In fact, the history of the Montanari family stretches back a great deal earlier than the Exhibition, although it was then that they first achieved fame. In the nineteenth century this family consisted of the following (their exact composition

190 *A portrait of Princess Beatrice, daughter of Queen Victoria, wearing an Arab burnous and clutching a doll. Painted by Winterhalter in 1859*

191 Opposite *A portrait doll of about 1864 representing the famous Swedish singer Jenny Lind, shown against a background of a biography and a contemporary picture. When she visited America in 1840 thousands of paper portrait dolls made in Germany were sold there*

192 Two small all-bisque French dolls with their original, beautifully made, and elaborate, clothes. These dolls, made in 1880, are only five inches tall

having been the subject of some confusion in the past): Madame Augusta Montanari, the mother who is listed in the London Post Office Directory in the 1850s as a 'model wax doll manufacturer', of 13 Charles Street, Soho Square, and her son Richard Napoleon Montanari, who is listed in the Directories of 1870 under 'doll-makers (wax)' and whose name in the list bears the dagger indicating a wholesale doll manufacturer. The husband of Augusta, Napoleon Montanari, appears in the same directories as his wife at the same address, but merely as 'Modeller' so that experts have now agreed that he was a modeller and sculptor in wax, rather than an actual doll-maker. The entries at the 1885 Paris Exhibition help to make the situation clear, for Augusta was given an award for wax dolls and Richard exhibited wax dolls and dolls' heads, whereas Napoleon merely exhibited wax figurines.

Tallis' classic description of the work of the Montanaris shows how in the field of wax dolls, in England, the Montanaris far outshone their competitors: 'The only exhibition of wax dolls that was deserving was one by Augusta Montanari to which a prize medal was awarded. The display of this exhibitor was the most remarkable and beautiful collection of toys in the Great Exhibition. It consisted of a series of dolls representing all ages from infancy to womanhood, arranged in

several family groups, with suitable and elegant model furniture. These dolls had the hair, eyelashes and eyelids separately inserted in the wax, and were, in other respects, modelled with life-like truthfulness. Much skill was also evinced in the variety of expression which was given to these figures in regard of the ages and stations which they were intended to represent.' Tallis goes on to comment on the high prices of the Montanari dolls – as much as five guineas undressed, and the dressed ones proportionately more expensive, a fact which is borne out by the comment of M. Henry d'Allemagne on the Paris World Exhibition of 1882: 'The wax dolls were of beautiful workmanship, but their prices were prohibitive for general trade.' A number of them were certainly exported to the United States.

Wax as a material had been known before the Montanaris, although they are deemed to have given it its finest expression. Wax was probably used in Italy at a very early date for making religious figures, and wax was also used at an early date for making funeral images in Europe. References to wax dolls, the products of Daniel Neuberger of Augsburg 'so marvellously coloured that they seemed alive' are found in Germany as early as the seventeenth century, and wax heads were moulded with elaborate hair styles for the fashion designers in France in the

193 An American Mammy doll of 1884 working at her stove with miniature pots and pans

194 A wax doll given by Queen Victoria in 1880 to Lady Esther Gore, later Viscountess Hambleden

195 **Opposite** *A bride doll made in the late nineteenth century, probably of French origin*

196 An illustration from a mid-nineteenth century child's alphabet book

eighteenth century. But before the Montanaris the use of wax poured into moulds had produced a certain monotony in the heads. In the early wax dolls, cheeks and lips were painted directly onto the surface, as were the eyebrows and eyelashes. Moving eyes were first used in England in about 1825 – the eyes opened and shut by means of a wire coming out of the body at the waist line, easily concealed by the voluminous dresses of the period. The later counter-balance system of shutting the eyes by a system of lead weights, used by most modern 'shut-eye' dolls, came in about 1870 and in the 1880s eyes moving from side to side were introduced, but they remained comparatively rare.

The Montanaris, with their beautiful and life-like dolls, were not, however, the only great family of doll-makers. The Pierotti family also made wax dolls, their dolls having particularly beautiful complexions, the wax being coloured by a secret process of their own, and the dolls having naturalistic curves, the curve of the neck being particularly effective on the baby dolls, having a curve of flesh at the back, and life-like creases at the necks and wrists. The bodies were generally of white calico, on to which the wax head and shoulders, arms and legs were carefully stitched.

The Pierotti family like the Montanaris, were part wax doll-makers, part wax modellers since the two trades were naturally allied. Doll-makers can be traced in this family as early as the 1780s when Domenico Pierotti first came to England from Italy, where according to some legends they had been making dolls since the 1100s. In 1862 Henry Pierotti is recorded as being a wax doll-maker who won a Bronze Medal at the International Exhibition for his dolls with inserted hair, while his daughter Celia exhibited foreign and English toys. The Pierotti family continued to supply the London toyshop of Hamley's with dolls up to 1930, a long history of co-operation.

Wax was not the only material popular in the nineteenth century: papier mâché, which literally means chewed paper, was also often used (figure 197). As an invention, it is ascribed by some to Italy and by some to France, while as early as the 1700s factories in England were turning out small articles made of paper pulp. Thereafter Germany took the lead in the making of papier mâché toys, although a quantity of dolls' heads of this material were made in America by the famous doll-maker Ludwig Greiner of Philadelphia. Greiner first patented them in 1858 and again in 1872, but as he is listed as a 'toy-man' in the Philadelphia directory as early as 1840, his work in America probably extended from the forties to the eighties.

Similar to papier mâché was composition, which was made of a mixture of many materials such as plaster of Paris, bran, sawdust and glue, and although malleable when wet, it hardened into a durable form. It appears to have been pioneered in England and later imitated in Germany. The composition surface of the face would be brightly painted and then waxed over in order to give the proper mellow look to the complexion.

Some collectors prefer the nineteenth-century china dolls, and their many variations, including Parian and bisque. Of course the harder nature of the material has enabled them to be preserved in a better state than their more fragile sisters in wax. As early as the fourteenth century, as we have seen, clay dolls were made in Augsburg, Nuremberg, and other places in Germany. Wherever there were suitable deposits of clay for making porcelain and china, dolls' heads were manufactured, the quality of the china depending not only on the quality of the clay, but also the fineness with which it had been ground.

Early porcelain dolls are very rare, although some prized dolls do exist from this

197 Priscilla, an early papier mâché milliner's model dressed by Eliza Mercer in 1835, with an interesting hairstyle of the period

period. The early German china heads are of a surprising variety of types, indicating that they were probably made in a number of different backyard kilns. During the nineteenth century, however, china heads became extremely popular, and it is often difficult to tell examples made early in the century from later models. Two clues worth following are that china heads with very steeply sloping shoulders are generally of an early date, and that the painted eyes of china heads in early models have a red line above them to denote the eye-lid.

The hair-style of the individual head is also often useful in dating it although one cannot rely on this indication too much, as the same mould was sometimes used after the hairstyle had gone out of fashion. It is interesting to find that though the eyes of china dolls are generally blue, the colour of the hair is nearly always black. As the Germans are famous as a blonde nation, presumably the artists were enamoured of the striking contrast between the black hair and the whiteness of the china.

Other china heads have an actual hole in the crown: German heads in particular favoured this, because it reduced the weight of the head and as the export of china

198 Punch and Judy figures of the late nineteenth century standing over a set of Punch and Judy postcards

heads from Germany was an enormous business, it was an advantage to pay a lower tariff charge on a lighter head. Once arrived at its destination abroad, the hollow head could be closed up with cardboard or composition to which the wig could then be attached.

Parian heads have been a source of some confusion to collectors. How do Parian heads differ from bisque heads? The answer is that all unglazed china heads are made of bisque, which is no more than a technical term for the biscuit mix, which constitutes china before it is fired. But certain unglazed heads were produced without any colouring matter at all and these dead white heads came to be known as Parian from their resemblance to the white marble from the Greek island of Paros. Heads with a moderate amount of colouring matter were known as 'blonde bisque' and highly coloured ones simply as 'bisque', while some rather coarse greyish heads were termed 'stone bisque'. Parian type China was invented by Spode and was a patent of the Spode factory from the 1840s. The hardness of the paste made it possible to cast a mould of great detail and delicacy, and the hair styles in particular show many variations with their braids, ringlets, plaits and curls. Parian heads, unlike china

199 An interior of a dolls' house, dated about 1865, formerly in Saltram House, Devon. The mahogany book cases and contents and the needlework carpet were part of the original furnishings. The rest is furniture of the same period, but was added to this particular house later. The globe is dated 1851

heads, are generally blonde. One type of miniature doll made of Parian was known as a 'Frozen Charlotte' after a heroine in an American ballad.

However, bisque stimulated finer examples of toy-making than Parian – some of the finest dolls' heads in existence were made out of bisque by the efforts of the Jumeau family firm in the years between 1844 and 1898. The Jumeaus are to bisque what the Montanaris are to wax. The early Jumeau doll heads were imported from Germany and were actually 'blonde bisque' in type; this probably explains why the Jumeau dolls were not praised for themselves but only for their exquisite gowns and undergarments at the Great Exhibition of 1851. In 1862 however, M. Jumeau decided to undertake the manufacture of his own doll-heads and it is these Jumeau heads which are universally agreed to be of a rare beauty, with their large, even over-size, soulful eyes, which were made of glass, looking exactly like artificial eyes for human beings. M. Jumeau's son also invented a swivel neck, which he patented in 1860. The bodies of the early dolls were generally made of kid on a wire foundation; later wood was used, to make a beautifully formed body jointed at the waist, elbows and ankles as well as in the usual places. However, this type of

200 *A baby doll in a cradle : the baby doll was a nineteenth century innovation Previously dolls had been dressed as adults, but the baby doll, once introduced, was immediately popular*

body was expensive to produce, and Jumeau's son is credited with the invention of a cheaper type of body of composition, strung together with elastic, a method which has continued up to the present day.

Rubber enjoyed a great popularity as a material after 1851 when the first rubber doll was made under patent for Goodyear. Rubber, with its unbreakable qualities, was obviously an ideal material for dolls actually handled and hugged by children, unlike wax or china.

The doll which had acted as a fashion emissary in the eighteenth century found another role in the nineteenth century as a form of 'fan photograph', for the nineteenth-century portrait dolls can certainly be compared to this twentieth-century phenomenon. First of all, one must distinguish between what is, and what is not, a portrait doll. The first figure to be widely celebrated in doll portraiture was Queen Victoria, both as a sovereign and a young princess before her accession. However, numerous dolls of the period, although clearly influenced by Queen Victoria's looks and hair style, were not intended to be actual portraits of her and were not sold as such. The youthful Victoria was graceful, and there are many charming examples of doll portraits of her in museums and private collections. Her coronation was the signal for a wave of such portraits; there is a particularly charming one in the Bethnal Green Museum, London, where the robes are very finely worked, and another example in the London Museum where the robes are less magnificent, but the face more life-like.

Queen Victoria's large family of nine children also provided models for the portrait artists. The rising popularity of wax resulted in some really delightful examples, notably a pair of children representing the Princess Royal and the Prince of Wales, and another portrait of the Prince of Wales in a tartan dress and a straw hat, all of them now in the London Museum. Both the beautiful Princess Alexandra, bride of the Prince of Wales, and the Empress Eugénie of France, inspired the makers at about the same date.

In America, Jenny Lind, the singer known as 'the Swedish Nightingale', was a most popular subject during her triumphal tour of the States. There is a particularly fine example in the collection of Miss Irene Blair Hickman in London. Jenny Lind's tour from 1850–1 was exceptionally well publicised, because her husband

was extremely commercially minded, and also because she was sponsored by P.T. Barnum, rightly termed the Prince of Showmen. The Jenny Lind dolls of the day were made in Germany; although the singer had blonde Scandinavian colouring, they nearly always show her with black hair, as she always wore a black wig on the stage (figure 191).

Other popular American portrait figures in the nineteenth century were George and Martha Washington, and the American presidents and their wives, notably Thomas Jefferson and Mary Todd Lincoln; these figures, perhaps not portraits in the contemporary sense of Queen Victoria and Jenny Lind, still fulfilled the same function of providing for popular admiration.

The nineteenth-century dolls' house is an enormous subject, for the houses are numerous and varied and, although perhaps they do not have the elegance of those of the eighteenth century, they certainly fall more surely into the category of toys. One feels much more confident that the nineteenth-century dolls' houses were actually used by children. Gone is the grandeur of the eighteenth-century dolls' house. Miniature silver is now replaced by china in the interior, and in consequence there are hooks on the houses instead of locks.

201 A wax Montanari doll of great beauty, about 27 inches tall. Her body is made of white calico to which the wax arms, legs and bust are attached. She wears a dress which was worn by a four-year-old child of this period, about 1865.

202 A fashion doll of the 1870s

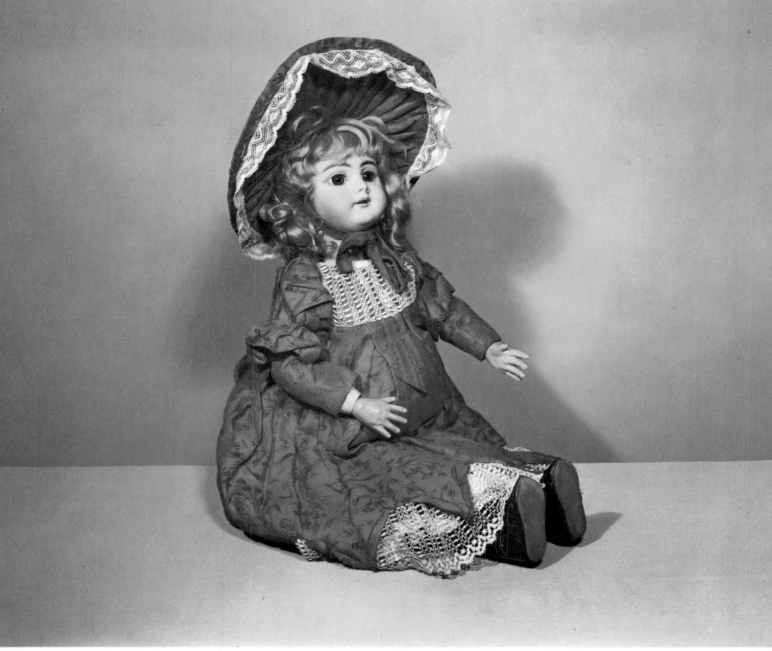

203 A walking doll of the late nineteenth century made by the famous Jumeau family in France

Between 1800 and 1830 a series of strong plain houses were manufactured. They were about 4 feet high and 3 feet wide, solidly made, and thinly painted to represent stone. They have three or four rooms, and no staircase. The front opens in one wing, and sometimes one side of the roof lifts up, or there is a drawer in the plinth for spare furniture. Dolls' houses are now being made commercially as well as at home. From the 1850s to the 1860s the interior is badly executed and meanly proportioned and in the 1870s the houses are smaller and the stand which had disappeared, returns, looking rather like a wash-stand.

At the same time the accoutrements for a dolls' house have become much more elaborate, and are being widely sold. After 1850 there were many toy bazaars in London which supplied them: the Lowther Arcade in London, stretching from West Strand to Adelaide Street and the Soho Bazaar were both rich sources for this type of toy and both are known to have sold mainly German and French toys. Another well known toyshop was Cremer of Regent Street, which was founded before 1830, and where Lewis Carroll used to take the small Greville Macdonald in the 1860s.

*204 A case of three early shell dolls,
eight inches high, made in the Channel
Islands in the 1830s*

Perhaps the most interesting of these accoutrements are the dinner services. A series of dinner sets was made in England by the use of transfers, in Staffordshire and Newcastle. China tea sets were imported into America from the 1800s, as only pottery and metal ones were made there. Pewter dishes were made widely in Nuremberg, both for dolls' houses and to furnish the Nuremberg kitchens. Leslie Daiken described the Nuremberg kitchen as a 'typical German attempt' to bring usefulness into doll play; but those of us who were given a modern version of these little kitchens as children will surely take a more kindly view. A glimpse into this tiny world, so open and candid to our gaze, yet so closed forever from our participation, is infinitely alluring, with the elusive magic of something glimpsed, yet unattainable. Glassware, which, as we have seen, had been known earlier, continued to be manufactured in miniature in Bohemia, and there was a passing vogue for miniature ivory furniture from China. The first really cheap ware was painted turned ware imported from Bavaria from the 1830s onwards.

However, one of the specialities of the nineteenth-century dolls' house was kitchenware, and all sorts of objects in miniature are found in the kitchen, including

205 *A collection of miniature clocks and lamps, made between 1840 and 1890, a bureau with an inset mirror, a davenport, candle-snuffer and table globe in the foreground, also a 'baccarat' paper weight. Dolls' houses were often elaborately furnished, with no detail overlooked*

206 *The nineteenth-century dolls' house often had miniature dinner services, complete with plaster food. Here is part of a Meissen dinner service, about 1860–5, with joint, spinach, tarts and other foods in plaster attached to the dishes. The peaches and melon are parts of other sets*

208 **Opposite** *A collection of articles for a dolls' house. Even miniature sheet music was printed for dolls' 'use'*

207 *A collection of dolls' boots and shoes of different periods between 1830 and 1860*

209 *A pedlar doll with her bazaar stall.*
English, about 1835

linen-presses, flat-irons, tin candle boxes, and salt and knife boxes. There is as much emphasis on food as on kitchens, as though the inhabitants of the nineteenth-century dolls' house were outstanding gourmets! The German toymakers in particular were famous for the food in their dolls' houses, so colourful and so pretty in design, as well as so lifelike, that it lights up the interior (figure 206); a great deal of attractive food is illustrated in the Biberach catalogues. One recalls the delicious food in Beatrix Potter's *Tale of the Two Bad Mice* and how the mice broke into the nice conventional red brick dolls' house occupied by Lucinda and Jane, and on finding the succulent ham and other foods were merely plaster, furiously broke them to pieces with shovel and firetongs. Certainly every child has experienced at one time or another a feeling of frustration, particularly, perhaps, at seeing the pink and white ice cream on the plaster slabs – even if he does not always express his feelings like the two bad mice.

From the 1840s onwards, lead imported from Germany to England was used for beds. Varnished birchwood furniture is said to have been made in Russian villages and collected by sledge each year for sale at the toy fairs of Leipzig and

210 Paper dolls from McLoughlin Brothers, New York, about 1870. They come from the Paper Doll Bridal Party *which also includes a bridesmaid*

Novgorod. Much of the imitation rosewood furniture which has survived is of the highest quality, and small masterpieces were produced in many designs and a number of different sizes, including chairs, bureaux and bookcases as well as occasional tables and a sewing table. Mrs Greene thus gives them their epitaph: 'They can be classified among the minor arts, part amateur in origin – shell arrangements, shadow pictures, tinsel prints – whose merit lies less in themselves than that they state the simplicities of their time.' And to this graceful epitaph one may add the knowledge of the pleasure given to children in a bygone nursery of a bygone day.

Nineteenth-century dolls were not only endowed with houses – mostly much too small for them to inhabit – they also had carriages. These are particularly attractive and many have survived thanks to their sturdy workmanship, particularly in large houses in the country, where they have been played with by succeeding generations of children. In the United States the toymaker Benjamin Potter Crandall sold baby carriages billed as 'the first baby carriages manufactured in America' in the 1830s for 1 dollar 50 cents. At first the carriage was a simple affair with two wheels and no rear axle. Later carriages were elegant four-wheeled affairs with springs and fringed tops, and a Crandall doll carriage with a leather hood made in 1867 may be seen in the Museum of the City of New York. The Crandalls were at work virtually throughout the century improving their carriages, as may be seen from the evidence of their many additional patents, including one which may well have been for the first folding carriage. The catalogue of the firm of Ellis, Britton & Eaton for 1866 shows as many as forty different carriages and perambulators. Also known as the Vermont Novelty Works, they made a toy gig for dolls with a top that folded back which sold 7,000 and a toy cart with a brightly painted body which sold over 6,000.

Dolls not only had carriages and houses, they also had elaborate trousseaux. One doll in the Essex Institute in Salem, Massachussetts has five complete costumes, a rubber hot-water bottle, a fan, hatbox, eyeglasses, a lorgnette, watch, gold cross on a chain, locket, two pairs of kid gloves, two pocket books, clothes brush, hairbrush and comb and a mirror!

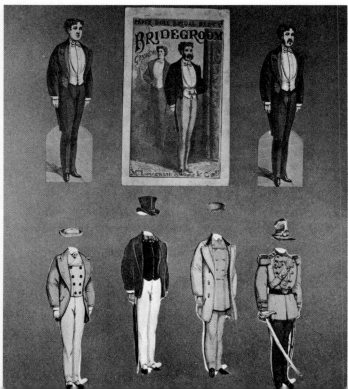

11 The Nursery before the First World War

When reading contemporary memoirs and reminiscences, one is tempted to think that nursery life in the years before the First World War must have been uniquely pleasant. The toys those golden children played with, some of which can still be found in the same nurseries, while others have found their way into the growing numbers of Toy Museums, have a special aura. Even the toys of the First World War itself, the soldier dolls and the model soldiers, the guns which remind one of the first great wave of belligerent feeling to sweep across the world for many years, have a certain glamour about them.

Perhaps the spirit of this carefree time is best conveyed by a study of H. G. Wells' little book on Floor Games, published in 1913. Here is no introspection about the British Empire, pacifism, what is or is not good for the children's souls, but a careless confidence that children play with what amuses them, and that this in turn must be the best possible thing for their future happiness (figure 210). Wells names four categories of toys – soldiers, bricks, boards and planks, and clockwork rolling stock and rails, all of which he deems an essential part of a happy child's life: he also finds a place for minor objects like tin ships, easter eggs and the like.

Planks are most important in his view, but were not stocked by the toyshops in 1913 (we shall see later what a profound effect this demand for planks in 1913 was to have on the British toy experts Paul and Marjorie Abbatt in the 1930s). Wells comments loftily: 'We don't as a matter of fact think much of toyshops. We think we trifle with great possibilities. We consider them expensive and incompetent and flatten our noses against their plate glass perhaps, but only in the most critical spirit.' With bricks, he waxes even more furiously against the toyshops . . . 'existing bricks are considered too small to make a decent home for even the smallest lead soldiers and there are never enough, never nearly enough.' At this point Wells gives what he considers the best dimensions for bricks, measurements which the Abbatts were to copy exactly in the thirties. In soldiers, Wells applauded recent improvements, what he described as 'the magnificent physique' of the new type of soldiers, and the appearance of movable arms, but deplores the lack of civilians – he adds 'I write now as if I were British Consul-General in Toyland, listing new opportunities for trade' – but we may wonder what he needed more civilians for, except as fodder for his massacres, and reflect on the unselfconscious bloodthirstiness of play before the holocaust of the 1914 War.

With regard to trains Wells regards a uniform gauge as absolutely essential – which surely experts would agree with – and he mentions that all his own trains are gauge O. Having thus reviewed the toy world of the turn of the twentieth century from the energetic masculine viewpoint, Wells turns to what is perhaps the most fascinating part of his book, his account of the games which are to be played, the Floor Games themselves. He describes one, the Game of Wonderful Islands; where the floor is the sea, full of wonderful archipelagos, with lyrical enthusiasm: 'We land and alter things and build and rearrange and hoist paper flags on pins, and

211 The rocking-horse was one of the favourite inhabitants of the pre-1914 nursery, recalled with love in many memoirs of the period

212 *A drawing from the* Illustrated London News *showing H.G.Wells playing some of the floor games which he described in his book on the subject published in 1913*

subjugate populations and confer all the blessings of civilisation upon these lands.'

The wonder and curiosity of the nursery in those days is also well expressed in Eleanor Farjeon's *Nursery in the Nineties*, published by the Oxford University Press. She describes the powerful part which Cremer's toyshop played in their lives: 'Harry's superb Noah's Ark came from Cremer's too. One night he launched it in his bath, and left it floating. Where it sailed to by night, who shall say? In the morning it held a cargo to delight a child. Whenever he left it hopefully afloat, his hopes in the morning were not disappointed. Above all, Dobbin came to us from Cremer's. He had two simple green rockers, and a brown hair coat. How we despised later on, the unreal varnished breed of rocking-horse with horizontal action back-and-forth instead of the authentic up-and-down! Dobbin was *real*, you fondled the ears and wore his smooth neck smoother still with kisses. One day we discovered that his horsehair tail pulled out. We explored his stuffing, as far as small fingers could poke. In the days to come we began to find "things" in Dobbin; like the Noah's Ark, he became a yielder of treasures. I recollect jewellery of the "Bong-Bong" order (we called your Christmas Crackers Bong-Bongs then).'

It is interesting that dolls are dismissed as things 'I never cared for' whereas a

213 The Clifford Berryman cartoon of 'Teddy' Roosevelt which inspired the Ideal Toy Corporation to making a teddy-bear

214 Two teddy-bears showing signs of long use and affection. That on the left is French and one of the earliest surviving teddy-bears and the one on the right is dated 1910

215 Bygones: *an evocative illustration of forgotten pre-war toys in an attic by Rosemary Howard, showing a French rocking-horse from the St Remy district of Provence*

tea-set was valued, not for dolls' tea parties but for the children's own tea-parties, which confirms the present writer's experience that children must be involved in their play, and in any given dolls' tea party the dolls are quickly edged away from the tea table, the tiny cups are soon no longer pressed to their lips, but to the children's with many a gracious explanation: 'Delicious tea, my dear! What grace! What goodness!' presumably in imitation of their parents' own manner.

One true companion of childhood hours made his first appearance during this period: this was the teddy bear (figure 214). What is it about the teddy bear which gives it this fantastic appeal for children? This is without doubt one of the most interesting psychological questions about the history of toys, why this not particularly unusual object should have this amazing and enduring hold on the affections of children, and should have survived many other passing fads. The origin of the teddy bear is in fact one of chance. The teddy bear first appeared in 1903, as the result of a cartoon which appeared in the Washington Post by Clifford Berryman (figure 213) after a photograph had been widely shown in the newspapers of Teddy Roosevelt after a bear hunt in the Rocky Mountains with a little brown bear

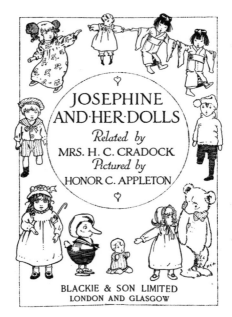

JOSEPHINE
AND·HER·DOLLS
Related by
MRS. H. C. CRADOCK
Pictured by
HONOR C. APPLETON

BLACKIE & SON LIMITED
LONDON AND GLASGOW

*216 The title page of this book,
published in 1915, illustrates the types of
doll a child played with at this time. Mrs
H.C.Cradock was the author and
Honor C. Appleton the illustrator of
this popular series of children's books*

lying at his feet. At that time there was a border dispute between Mississippi and Louisiana and when the President was on a hunting trip in Mississippi and refused to shoot a bear cub which crossed his line of fire, this appeared as a political cartoon, captioned 'Drawing the line in Mississippi'.

On seeing the Berryman cartoon, Morris Michtom, founder of the American toy firm Ideal Toy Corporation, wrote to the President, whom he had always admired, and asked whether it would be an impertinence for him to make a small bear cub and call it 'Teddy's bear'. According to Mr Ben Michtom, son of the founder, and the present President of the Ideal Toy Corporation, Theodore Roosevelt wrote back to Mr Michtom, saying in effect: 'I don't think my name is worth much to the toy bear cub business, but you are welcome to use it.' Mrs Michtom was deft with the needle and herself helped to make many of the samples of this bear, one of which was sent to the President, and others taken with the President's letter to Mr Schoonmaker, then buyer of the large wholesaler, Butler Brothers. In 1903 Butler Brothers took the entire output of these teddy bears, and guaranteed Mr Michtom's credit with the mills, who supplied him with the plush. This incidentally was the beginning of what was later to be called the Ideal Toy Corporation, as well as the birth of the teddy bear. When Mr Michtom died in 1938, Theodore Roosevelt's widow, Edith, wrote to his widow, offering condolences on the passing of the man who made the teddy bear famous.

The teddy bear, although of strictly American origin, was also manufactured in large numbers in Germany at the same period (the early German bears had much longer and thinner limbs than the teddies of today) notably by the Steiff Company. The teddy bear had another off-shoot: in 1962 the U.S. Government authorised the Ideal Toy Corporation to make Smokey the Bear, the symbol of Forest Fire Prevention, as a tribute to the fact that they had invented the teddy bear. The following clause appeared in the licence given to them by the Government: 'The licensee may attach to the Smokey Bear stuffed animal a detachable Jr. Forest Ranger Badge approved by the Forest Service.' This badge thus implies that every child wearing it is a Government agent dedicated to the conservation of American forests. The Smokey Bear is one of the endless permutations of the ever popular teddy, of which another prototype is illustrated, the poet Mr John Betjeman's teddy bear 'Archie' (figure 5).

We have seen H. G. Wells' views on soldiers 'increasingly magnificent'. Certainly in the last years before the 1914 War soldiers were developed a great deal, particularly by William Britain. Up till 1893 England had looked primarily to Germany for her toy soldiers, particularly to Allgeyer of Fürth, later Heinrichsen and later Heyde as noted in chapter 10. William Britain insisted on a uniform gauge, in the way that Wells commended, related to the then fashionable uniform gauge of railways. Up to this point trains had been the most popular masculine nursery game, but Britain's developments in soldiers – to the extent that whereas in 1895 there were twenty varieties, by 1905 there were five million castings in over a hundred varieties – meant that soldiers succeeded trains.

The effect of the 1914 War on the use of soldiers in the nursery was, as might be expected, to encourage the martial spirit; at the same time the rise of pacifism meant that certain children were not allowed soldiers at all. Also the shortage of raw materials meant that production slowed up to a certain extent although Henry Harris remembers seeing British redcoats in the toyshops of Dublin, even in 1916.

Some people were naturally concerned about the popularity of war games, which they felt to be inappropriate while the world was searching for peace. One preacher devoutly hoped that someone would invent a 'peace toy' that would be as exciting and interesting as war toys.

The American Soldier Company, however, took a forceful view to the contrary. As manufacturers of toy soldiers, forts, military camp scenes, they sent to the retail trade a little booklet entitled *Good Reasons for NOT Buying Military Games*. The pages of the booklet were completely blank. Milton Bradley at the same period made a stirring war game called 'At the Front' which was described in part as follows: 'The box contains soldiers which are to be taken out and fired at, for which deadly purpose there are pistols enough for considerable execution. Each soldier stands till he is shot and then falls like a man and takes no more part in the game. The uniforms are of the latest and most correct styles, representing armies of different countries.'

In an article in the 50th Anniversary issue of the British magazine *Games and Toys*, Mr Sidney Myers of L. Rees & Co reflected from the depths of his experience on the toy most popular in 1914. He chose the mechanical train sets – that is to say clockwork for the masses, and a few mechanical train sets for the rich. In his view

217 A soldier doll in the uniform of the 1914–18 war

218 A Cossack doll, made in Germany in 1914

219 A British clockwork train created by one of the most inventive people in the British toymaking industry, Frank Hornby – the man who also invented the Meccano system. Clockwork trains were much cheaper than electrical ones and were produced for the mass market

nowadays the miniature gauge or table railway, both clockwork and electric, has largely usurped the position of the once popular O gauge. But then not only clockwork trains, but clockwork cars were becoming increasingly popular, and not only cars, but also fire engines, road rollers, buses and tram cars, delivery vans, and many other similar toys.

Mr Myers particularly recalls the motley and wide range of dolls enjoyed in 1914, including leather and leather-stuffed cambric, all of which, except the wax dolls, had porcelain heads. The filling of soft toys in those days was wood wool, although some of the better toys were stuffed with kapok. The material used to cover them was generally mohair plush, and washability – that marvellous watchword of the modern mother in choosing a soft toy for her child – was unheard of.

It is interesting that Mr Myers draws attention to the popularity of dolls in England in 1914. The same point is born out by an extract from the American magazine *Playthings* in 1903, which reports an unprecedented demand for dolls, continuing during these years up to the First War. Baby dolls are reported to be selling better than ever, and serviceable dolls have kid bodies and real hair. There are dolls' corsets of different sizes and colours, and even dolls' hammocks, to say

nothing of one of the newest items – a dolls' shower bath. A garage at the same period is touchingly described as an 'automobile livery stable', and reported as attracting considerable attention in the stores. *Playthings* adds rather charmingly: 'Perhaps the proper name for this would be "garage" as that is the name given to an automobile station by enthusiastic motorists'. Other new toys reported are an electric telephone, selling at 7 and 10 dollars, baseball games and jockey sets.

While the garage or automobile livery station belongs to the future (for in the 1960s what little boy does not have a garage for his endless small elegant and cheap mini-cars?) the doll of the 1900s definitely belongs to the past. In this period, however, other makers came to the fore, to join the names we have already considered in the last chapter. One of the many doll-makers who achieved eminence at the turn of the twentieth century was a German named Armand Marseille who produced baby dolls of particular charm. His dolls were marked by his initials and a number, usually on the back of the neck or just underneath the hair, and as any doll which came into England after 1908 had to be stamped with the country of its origin, Armand Marseille dolls often bear the words 'Made in

220 A doll in the robes of a peeress, made at the time of the coronation of King George V in 1910

221 A well-made dolls' house of about 1880, with four rooms, hall and curving stair. It has been painted and furnished as a market-town hotel by the present owner

Germany' in addition to their other marks. Early Armand Marseille dolls had jointed kid bodies; by 1908 and 1909 their bodies were often of pink canvas with bisque lower arms, while the legs were simply stuffed to imitate black stockings. By 1911 there were many examples of dolls with wooden bodies, arms and legs, the arms and legs below the knee being covered with composition. Nearly all of them had eyes which open and shut, the eyelids being part of the eyeball as in most dolls of this period.

The Armand Marseille dolls although perhaps cheaper than the Jumeaus were still dolls in the grand manner. But another type of doll of a very different sort was developed at this time, more modern in conception and in a line of development which leads right down to the Beatles' mascot toys of the present day. The golliwog, mentioned earlier, is one of the earliest examples. The golliwog first broke upon the world in 1895 in Florence Upton's delightful children's best seller *The Adventures of Two Dutch Dolls and a Golliwogg* (figure 226). Florence Upton was apparently inspired by some grotesque dolls belonging to her grandmother, which had been put away for years. This first book was followed by a number of others in the same

222 A car of about 1910, possibly made by the carpenter on a private estate

series, all celebrating the golliwog. As a result it was eagerly reproduced by toy-makers and became a familiar inhabitant of the nursery.

Psychologists sometimes question the giving of golliwogs to young children on the grounds that the black face, pop eyes and big red mouth are the unconscious source of many childish nightmares. Lady Mary Clive, describing her Edwardian childhood in *A Day of Reckoning*, certainly gives a horrifying picture of the giant child-size golliwog which her mother bought for her eldest brother, and which was universally feared by the children, who preferred the more welcoming and cosy teddy bear. Clearly there is some frightening element in the golliwog, and it may not be every child's favourite. It contains something of the grotesque element which we have traced in toys throughout the ages. But this grotesque element in toys does call forth a positive response in many children, who have a marked propensity for toys or even books that frighten them, and will actually demand to be read 'that book – the one that frightens me'. Clearly then children find a sort of *angstliebe* in the grotesque, to which the golliwog presumably appeals, and this accounts for its instant popularity after the publication of Florence Upton's book.

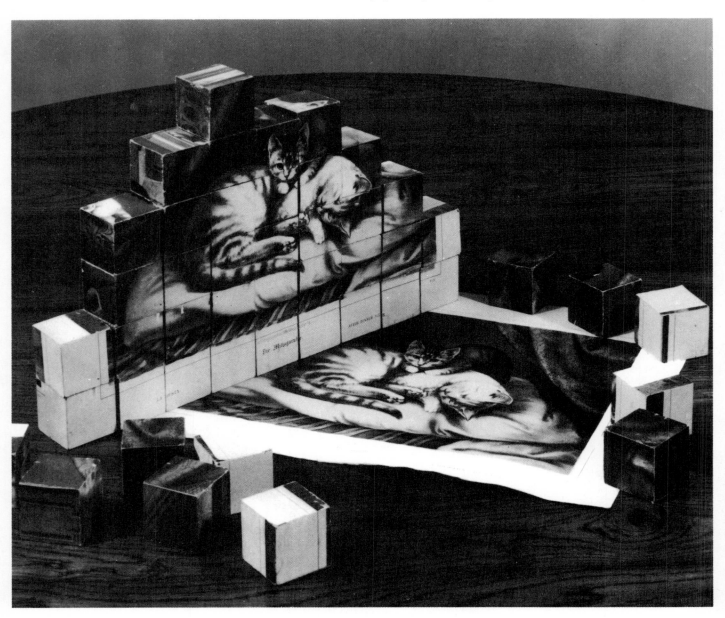

224 a and b Two illustrations from Dean's Rag Books Catalogue 1912–13, showing the patriotic spirit abroad on the eve of the First World War. These books were first produced in 1903 by a man who envisaged a really indestructible book for children on the grounds that they 'wear their food and eat their clothes'. These rag books enjoyed, and still enjoy enormous success all over the world

Other mascot dolls and toys to enjoy popularity at this period are dolls in America based on popular motion picture comedians, for example the John Bunny dolls made by Louis Akberg & Son. Strobel & Wilkin Company offered five characters from Little Nemo, Winsor McCay's popular cartoon series. Mutt and Jeff standing and walking dolls were also popular.

Among the dolls which featured in the wave of grotesque dolls was Billiken, a stiff little statuette, which was put on the market in 1909 with a Can't Break head, and a series of costumes, also a little rhyme which rather touchingly concluded:

> I love obedient girls and boys
> I am the king of all the toys.

Another grotesque doll was called Sunny Jim, produced by E. I. Horsman, who also produced Baby Bumps, perhaps the first doll to be sculpted from a real baby, and then Negro Baby Bumps. The Campbell kids, a cross between an advertisement gimmick and a mascot toy, were produced by arrangement with the famous soup company in 1907. My own favourite is Patty Comfort, the doll with

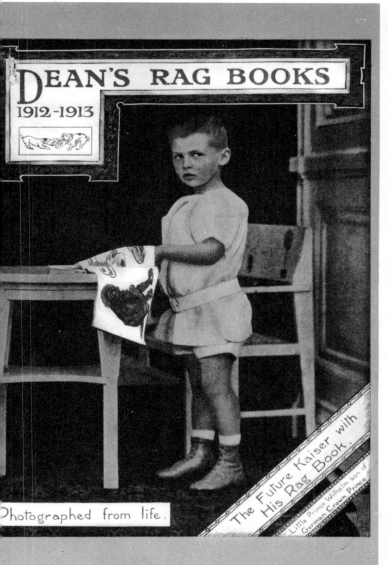

DEAN'S RAG BOOKS
1912-1913

Photographed from life.

The Future Kaiser with His Rag Book.
Little Prince Wilhelm son of German Crown Prince

Dean's Patriotic Pinafores for Children.

"I'M THE OFFICER!"
This 'ittle officer is wearing one of "Dean's Patriotic Pinafores".
Photographed from life.

AWARDED A GOLD MEDAL, FESTIVAL OF EMPIRE EXHIBITION, 1911.
9

225 A set of wooden stocks of various nursery rhyme characters

the hot-water bottle inside her, an early prefiguration of the popular telephone dolly of the 1920s, who was patented in 1907, and presumably made a most warm and desirable night-time companion for a child. She was accompanied, in her case, by the following endearing jingle:

> Patty Comfort's a rubber lined dolly
> To hug any other were folly
> When filled full of air
> She's light and she's fair
> And filled with hot water she's jolly.

The Kewpie dolls, with their strange almost lewd appearance, were another sympton of the same trend. Rose O'Neill had been drawing her top-knotted babies, with verses and stories, for the *Ladies Home Journal* for some years, and as they were very popular, they were obviously an ideal subject for toys. The first Kewpie dolls, of bisque, were made in Germany, but within a short while great numbers, both authorized and unauthorized versions, were being made in America in celluloid.

226 An illustration from The Adventures of Two Dutch Dolls and a Golliwogg *by Florence Upton. First published in 1895, this book introduced the golliwog to the world*

The Edwardian dolls' house, in the eyes of the experts, seems to decline slightly from the high standard set in the eighteenth century, and whereas the Victorian dolls' houses were well built, if not always elegant, the Edwardian ones have thin walls and the houses are made often of bad wood. They have unpleasantly proportioned rooms and the kitchen always seems to be the largest room in the house. At the same time the natural inventiveness of the turn of the century affected dolls' houses. Flora Gill Jacobs has done valuable research in the American patent office on this aspect of the dolls' house, discovering such treasures as a dolls' house with a lift, patented in 1899. A great many patentors seem to have been

obsessed with collapsible buildings, and one-room dolls' houses are especially in evidence, as well as collapsible houses, which in Flora Gill Jacobs' words are 'affairs which possess all household advantages including veranda and bath, but can be knocked down and shipped by a manufacturer with a minimum of bulk, eternal bugbear of the commercial dolls' house'.

The Schönhut toys were among the most popular at this period (figure 239). The Schönhut story is an interesting one, and shows the triumph of German enterprise allied to American markets and development. Albert Schönhut came to America from Germany right after the Civil War, and went to work in Philadelphia for John Deiser & Sons, toy jobbers and importers. Among the playthings brought from Germany were toy pianos, which were not then made in the States and which often arrived in a state of disrepair. Schönhut was clever at mending these pianos, and eventually set himself up in business in 1872, turning from pianos to musical toys, and after the turn of the century to a series of different toys, not necessarily connected with music. His Humpty Dumpty Circus, for example, was one of the most popular toys of its period; it consisted of a circus of performing animals and clowns with really moveable joints. You could pose one clown so that he kicked another; you could make an elephant stand on its hind legs, put a clown in the middle of a somersault, balance the lady horseback rider on her galloping steed, so that children could give full rein to their fantasies and take an active part in play with this toy.

According to Inez Marshall and McClintock in their extensive work *Toys in America*, Albert Schönhut never knew who had actually invented the Humpty Dumpty Circus, for an anonymous gentleman came into the firm one day with the invention, and refused to accept a royalty for it, taking merely 100 dollars outright payment, in spite of Schönhut's protestations that he should take more. The story has it, that the man merely wanted enough money to leave his wife, whom he loathed, and 100 dollars was therefore sufficient to solve the only problem he had.

In May 1903 a double page spread in *Playthings* announced 'The Humpty Dumpty greatest show on earth' selling from 1 to 4 dollars, depending on the number of figures in each set. The development of these joined figures led Schönhut naturally on to the development of his jointed doll. His grandfather had carved wooden dolls in Germany in 1796 but Schönhut's jointed wooden dolls in America were made by much advanced techniques.

In 1901 England saw the patenting of one of the great standbys of the English boyhood – the Meccano system – which sprang from the inventive brain of Frank Hornby, creator of Hornby Trains and one of the great names in toy-making on two fronts. Frank Hornby began life working in the office of a Liverpool firm of importers, where he rose to be chief managing clerk, and took to making toys in order to meet the demands of his young sons. The idea of Meccano came to him from watching a crane at work, when he was struck by the essential simplicity of the idea, and it occurred to him that models could easily be made out of a small number of simple parts. Although he found it easy enough to make such a model out of parts and nuts and bolts, it is curious to reflect on the extraordinary difficulties he found in persuading manufacturers to take up his invention – considering the boundless pleasure it was to give to children, and profit to its manufacturers. The early name of the toy was Mechanics Made Easy, but in 1907 this was changed to Meccano.

It would be wrong to conclude any consideration of toys before the First World War without mentioning aeroplanes and flying, which were developed during this

227 One of the earliest models of an aeroplane, made in 1904. Model aeroplanes were enjoyed by the public before the machines themselves had actually flown

period. In 1905 Milton Bradley's catalogue shows flying machines, and illustrated here is an early aeroplane (figure 227). Obviously among mechanical toys at that period, aeroplanes had the same position then as space toys do now, and offered a great deal of excitement to boys. Even before the aeroplane was a practical proposition, Penaud produced and sold flying models in the Paris shops – one of which, taken back by an uncle, was said to have been a source of inspiration to the Wright brothers as boys.

Soon after the Wright Brothers' first flight, toymakers began to manufacture some kind of toy flying machines. Milton Bradley's catalogue described 'an excellent imitation of the modern machines for navigating the air'. The Sears Roebuck catalogue of 1909 listed a 'Mechanical Flying Machine – fastened on a string it will fly round the room in a most natural manner'. The aeroplane was definitely a toy which pointed towards the future.

12 Toy-making as an Industry

228 *An early twentieth-century Bavarian tin toy of two moving cyclists*

229 Opposite *A German constructional toy, 1830–40, resting on its original box together with the accompanying toy catalogue of the Nuremberg firm of Biberach illustrating an almost similar toy*

The rise of toy-making as an industry is a mysterious process. Its history has seldom been charted, and most toymakers have been too busy making their toys to keep records. The same toy appears and disappears in different forms and in different countries in a manner which is confusing to the historians. At best the story of toys as an industry can only be sketched lightly. However, throughout this chapter it will be noticed that the graph of the toy trade advances in curves which are less dramatic than the actual economic trends of the time – a depression in trade is marked by a certain depression in the sale of toys, but a less profound one. There is something in the deep roots of the toy trade, extending far into the affections of its young customers, which enable it to survive economic crises with enviable stability.

Perhaps the family aspect of the toy trade has also something to do with it. Mr W.H.Lines, a respected figure in the British toy trade, whose firm has held a Royal Warrant for over a hundred years, recently commented on the number of family firms in the toy trade and defined what he called a 'toy man', who needs to have an instinctive knowledge of the mysteries of the trade. He mentions that in an age when international barriers are breaking down, a toy to succeed, must succeed all over the world, so presumably a toy man must be very conscious of the international potential of a toy, and not simply of its possibilities in the home market.

Toyshops as well as toymakers play their part in this particular web of history. Indeed for a child the toyshop is as much the progenitor of a toy as its maker, of whose existence he has but a dim idea. Many of one's earliest memories consist of fabulous visits to toyshops at Christmas with the magic instructions: 'Choose what you want. . . .' Then followed a tour of anguish and ecstasy – ecstasy at the choice, anguish at the need to make it.

The country in which toy-making first began to develop as an industry, far in advance of anywhere else, was Germany. Karl Gröber, asked why so many primitive folk toys seemed to have been started in Germany, claimed that museums support the theory of the German origin of most folk toys. It is indeed interesting to consider what it is in the German, or perhaps Central European character, which makes their folk toys so especially satisfying. But as Gröber pointed out, although the German toys were numerous, and the centres of toymaking many and vigorous, until 1800 it is difficult to have any clear picture of what occurred after the toy left the carver or agent's hand. By the end of the eighteenth century the seller was beginning to get into direct touch with his customers by means of catalogues and price lists, with illustrations, were also beginning to be used. Of the catalogues of the big houses, the most famous are those of Bestelmeier of Nuremberg, which contain over 1,200 different entries (figure 230). We notice how toys often survive from earlier ages, as for example Hilpert figures from the Rococo period, which were still being copied and sold much later. The new optical toys and mechanical toys were beginning to mingle with dolls and dolls' rooms and other toys which had played their part in the previous centuries.

230 *A page from a toy catalogue of*
Bestelmeier of Nuremberg. Bestelmeier,
one of the largest toy-houses in Germany,
used to have over 1,200 different entries
in its catalogue

Although Bestelmeier claimed that all the toys in his catalogue had been made by Nuremberg craftsmen (since toys made abroad were not allowed to be sold in Nuremberg) the illustrations in the catalogue show that much was offered which appears also in the catalogues of the Sonneberg and Gröden carvers. Printed and illustrated catalogues became more and more common and by the year 1850 every large speciality shop was issuing one. Means of distribution were becoming easier, and at the same time the restrictions noted earlier, which would only allow workers to manufacture within the strict limits of the regulations of their guild, were being slackened, and the time was passing when various trades, like cabinet makers and colourers, were not allowed to encroach on each other.

As the functions began to run together, so toy factories gradually came into being. The new workers were as much hand workers as their predecessors had been, but stood in a lower relation to the guild than the earlier hand workers. The disposal of toys was carried on as before, through an agent, until factories which organized the sale of their own toys were developed and the true competitive element, which is an essential part of every industry, was born. No longer did the

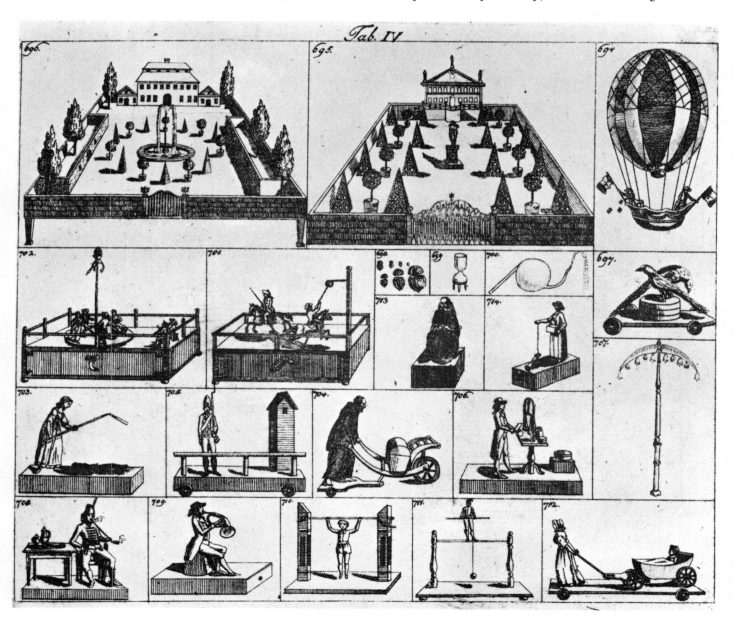

231 Painted tin steam boat 'Excelsior' made in America in the nineteenth century. An example of a native American toy as opposed to a copy of a European counterpart

guilds keep down the number of workers in any one town – each proprietor could make what he wished and could engage as many hands as he chose.

The German toy industry then was the scene of the transformation of folk art into an enormous industry. Although the advent of machinery meant that a certain standardization set in, because the Nuremberg centre to which the peasant craftsmen brought their crafts was anxious to please their customers in France, Russia, Great Britain, the Netherlands and the United States, as long as hand-skills were used, the toys never gave the feeling or appearance of being mass-produced. Later the advent of machinery was a limiting factor as far as originality in craftsmanship was concerned, but these German toys were noted for their sturdy construction, their beauty of design, their bright colours and their over-all eye appeal, which made children everywhere love them.

In the Gröden valley in the South Tyrol, a toy centre developed from which came more than three hundred skilled carvers, each specializing in one or several objects – this remote valley known as the Toy Valley had agents in more than one hundred cities on the Continent, and yet the population of the area comprised only 3,500

232 Broadway and 4th Avenue stage coach. A painted tin toy made by the Stevens and Brown Manufacturing Co. about 1870

people. As the industry grew and higher tariffs were imposed, the home toy industry was seriously affected, and the making of toys in these great centres dwindled. A substitute for wood, made of dough and lime pressed into moulds, gave an opportunity for making cheaper toys, but although this process, known as *drücken* or squeezing, made for increased production, the toys were not very durable. Then the toymakers turned to papier mâché, which was especially suitable for dolls' heads.

In the Erzegebirge in Saxony, toymaking replaced the mining industry during the eighteenth century. It is interesting to note that the playthings made there were primitive in design, deliberately aimed to stimulate the imagination of the children. As a result they became extremely popular as objects of barter among the Africans, and also in the Indies. Despite economic change and mechanization, the making of toys in this area has remained a home industry, and American merchants who visited the places where glass toys were made at Lauscha in Thüringen, in Bohemia and at Passau marvelled at the skill of blowers, often working under primitive conditions.

At the beginning of the twentieth century toy manufacturing was one of

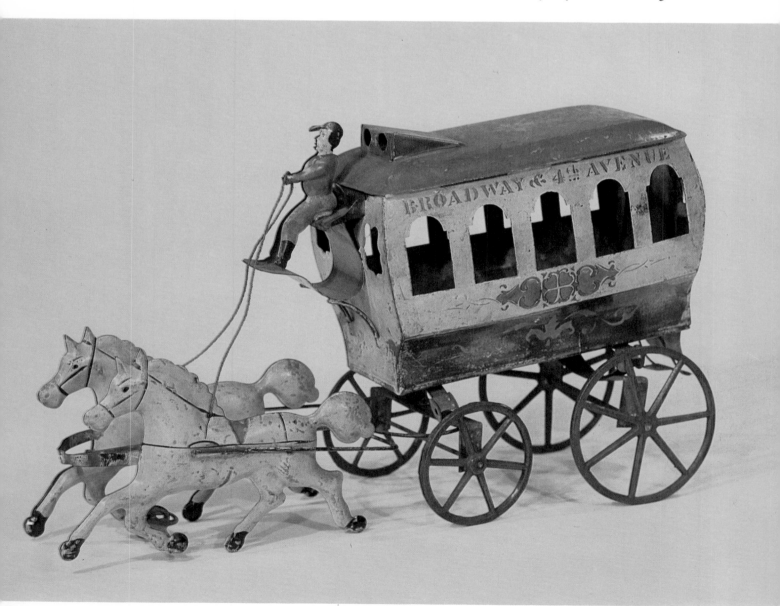

233 An early toy car, probably made in America

Germany's most important industries, and one fourth of the toys produced there were exported to the United States. One envisages the strange contrast of simple families, often four generations working under one roof for example in Sonneburg, in the Thuringian mountains, turning out from this unsophisticated environment toys intended for American children thousands of miles away in the clear bustling atmosphere of the New World.

The pattern of the American toy industry is however rather different and although folk toys were made in America, too, as we have seen, particularly in North Carolina, it has less deep roots than the German toy industry. The American industry only really developed when the tendency to import toys from Europe was conquered – throughout the eighteenth century the toys of the rich in America tended to come from Europe, and in the nineteenth century too, toys were imported from Europe on a vast scale. At the same time there *did* exist indigenous toys, and from 1840 onwards, contrary to popular belief, a true American home toy industry developed. Nor were all the toys copies of European models, in spite of the fact that European toys were the dominating influence.

From the 1840s onwards tin toys were being manufactured although the real advance occurred after the Civil War. There are distinguished names among old American toymakers such as Weeden, Stevens, Althof Bergman, Beggs, Carlisle and Finch, and Ives, mentioned earlier. All these made trains, iron and tin toys, steam toys, clockwork and electric toys, although a collector sometimes has difficulty in dating them, for example when a manufacturer has reproduced an ancient design. In the same way in 1947 the 'Surrey with the fringe on top' was reproduced after the fantastic success of the musical *Oklahoma*, which may well be misleading to collectors in later years. Louis Hertz regards tin toys as the oldest traceable American toy industry, for as early as the 1840s Turners of Meriden, Connecticut, began to utilize scraps for toys. The industry spread rapidly to New York and Philadelphia, and by the 1870s a single factory could produce between 40 and 50 million toys a year; among tin toys were dolls' furniture, musical instruments, kitchens, locomotives, bell toys and clockwork toys, and they tended to be finished in bright japanned colours. All these tin toys, produced at home in America, were similar to products made in France in the 1870s and then imported into America. However, American 'home-made' trains can be easily identified from foreign imported ones, because they have I, II and III on the carriages to denote the class.

Cast-iron was first widely used by American manufacturers in the later 1870s, except for oddments like banks, but in the 1880s extensive lines of iron toys were made, especially pull toy locomotives, and iron trains continue to flourish in the 1920s – it is universally agreed that the finest iron toys were those made by the Ives Company between 1868 and 1932. But American manufacturers did extremely well with their clockwork toys between 1865 and 1900, and elaborate French clockwork models never seriously presented competition.

The earliest surviving examples of wooden toys date from the Civil War, and from the Civil War to 1900 enormous numbers of wooden toys were decorated with brightly coloured lithographs and embossed pictures. Alphabet blocks, either cut out, embossed or lithoed, were extraordinarily popular.

234 Toy drums made in America in the late nineteenth century. Manufacturers were quick to benefit from the public interest in the Wild West – with drums, bows and arrows, wigwams, war toys, etc.

235 American nineteenth century rocking horse, with a 'snow' or 'fly' net cover

236 *A toy manufacturer's advertisement in the* Maine Business Directory *of 1856*

BRADFORD KINGMAN,
MANUFACTURER OF

CHILDREN'S CARRIAGES,
TOY WAGONS, SLEDS, ROCKING HORSES,

WHEELBARROWS, CABS, BUREAUS,
BEDSTEADS, FANCY BOXES, PORTABLE DESKS, TOY PAILS, &C.

SADDLE-TREES MADE TO ORDER AT SHORT NOTICE.
ALSO, MEDICINE CHESTS.
BOX SHOOKS CONSTANTLY ON HAND FOR SHIPPING.

The above Cuts represent some of the articles manufactured at this Establishment.
ALL ORDERS PROMPTLY ATTENDED TO.

237 *A paper duck, six inches long, made in America in the present century. It has a free moving head, carved wooden beak and feathers*

239 Opposite *From the Humpty Dumpty Circus of Schönhut, made in America and first sold there in 1903. For a quarter of a century this remained one of the most popular toys. All the figures were of wood and were held together by elastic cords, allowing a great variety of movement*

238 *A modern reproduction of a German folk toy of 1795, showing a bride's wedding cupboard with a doll of the period*

But the real boom in the American toy industry came with the First World War. In 1903 *Playthings*, the national magazine of the Toy Trade of the USA, was founded by Robert H. McCready – the first issue was only eighteen pages, but it grew rapidly in advertising volume and circulation, and by 1914 the American toy industry had expanded so much that issues of 100 pages were produced. The magazine underwent a period of further development in the 20s and 30s, and is today a fascinating monument to the enormous volume of the American toy trade and industry. Nowadays it publishes a special February pre-Toy Fair issue, then a March Toy Fair issue, and also an annual *Playthings* Directory issue, which is an encyclopedia of the American Toy Industry. All this is a far cry from the eighteen-page issue of 1903, but it is significant of the way in which the American toy trade has grown to gargantuan proportions. Robert McCready told Mr Voorhees, one of the pillars of the American toy world, that many people thought he was slightly crazy to establish a trade paper in an industry that had less than 100 manufacturers – for sixty years ago a high percentage of the toys sold in America were imported from Germany. Robert McCready was still editor of *Play-*

240 A modern Japanese display doll holding a warrior's head. The hands, face and feet are made of white cotton material

things when he died in 1951, a remarkable instance of a long reign: yet long reigns appear to be the rule not the exception in the toy world, and recently the British magazine *Games and Toys* celebrated its 50th anniversary under the same editor.

Almost immediately after the start of the First World War, imports from Germany were cut off, with the result that the American toy industry grew even more rapidly. The 1920s and 30s saw further growth, although like every other industry, it suffered in the depression years prior to the Second World War. But the growth and expansion of the American toy industry following the Second World War has been quite fantastic – the toy business in America has practically quadrupled in the last twenty years and toys have become what can only be described as a major industry. Toy sales in the United States are currently running close to two billion dollars at retail or about one billion dollars at manufacturers' prices. *Playthings* estimated that by 1914 half the toys used by American children were made in America and the rest came from Germany. The wartime embargo on German merchandise encouraged the American industry to capitalize on this opportunity by initiating revolutionary changes in toy designs, which were to supersede the traditional German toys.

The American Toy Association, known as Toy Manufacturers of the USA Inc, was founded in 1916 – earlier attempts to organize the American toy industry in this way having failed, because they were founded on restriction and price maintenance. This Toy Association went from strength to strength, sponsoring the Toy Fair in 1931 'to provide best climate for buyer and seller' and later a Toy Institute, which defines the basis for the wise selection of toys for children of different ages and interests. It has also from time to time sponsored enquiries into the state of the toy trade, such as *How to Sell Toys* in 1949, and the more sociological *Toy Purchase Habits of US Families* in 1954.

During the First World War, nationalistic feeling rose to such a point that some mothers actually destroyed toys with the 'Made in Germany' label on them, a phenomenon also observed in Britain in the Second World War with toys marked 'Made in Japan'. Shipping all over the world was interrupted, especially German and Italian. At this point naturally Japanese cheap toys saw their opportunity to come into the market, but after the war emphasis on quality curtailed their market. By 1924 there was a tremendous upsurge of interest in America in the whole subject of toys, including numbers of articles in journals emphasizing the need for quality in toys and the American quality market was able to a certain extent to drive out cheap Japanese toys. Congress also passed import duty laws to counteract the declining value of the German mark and allow US firms to compete with the foreign market. At the same time dyes were developed in the United States for use in toy manufacture in place of German aniline dyes.

Naturally in the thirties the industry was hit by the depression; but it clearly cannot have been too seriously affected, as the New York Toy Fair was actually founded in 1931, which would have hardly been the case had the toy industry been sunk in the economic doldrums. It has been estimated that by 1939 95% of American toys were manufactured at home, compared to 50% in 1914. The Second World War again brought a natural interruption of the trend, when armaments replaced peaceful pursuits, and the metal, rubber and chemical industries became top priority. There were natural developments like dolls being stuffed with sawdust and having cotton wigs instead of imported material, but the interest was certainly not totally destroyed and increased again after the war. Even in 1958, a so-called year of recession, Milton Bradley had its best-ever year for profits.

241 A collection of Shirley Temple dolls, showing the manufacturers' aptitude for playing on popular fancies by making mascot dolls based on famous stars. Shirley Temple was born in 1929, and first appeared in films in 1933. Her popularity was such that the Shirley Temple doll reached a sale of 1,500,000 in 1934

The reflections of Mr Charles S. Raizen, founder of the great Transogram American firm, at its 50th anniversary in 1965, sum up the attitude of the industry.

The memory of those far off beginning days, viewed in the light of the progress made by our industry through the years, and our present far reaching activities, suggest the realm of the fairy tale. I recall Transogram's small start and the endless tasks performed by Hawkings, the jack of all trades handyman, by Eddie, the ever busy office boy, and my own driving ambitions. It would seem as if we three performed every needed function of our little business . . .

To conceal the smallness of our three man executive crew, Eddie was always diffident about delivering the goods he had sold, and the Boss was not above carrying in those packages, and I too always managed to be busy on the off-side of the horse when Hawkings was carrying in the toys on the orders I had sold.

The progress Transogram has made in this half century is in measure reflected in the development of the toy industry in America during these years. In 1914 the amount of toys manufactured yearly in this country amounted to about 14 million dollars. This sum, I should like to mention with pardonable pride, is about what Transogram alone did in 1964.

French toymaking follows a more luxurious pattern than that of America. Whereas a feature of the growth of the American toy industry has been its fantastic rise in turnover – leading also to fantastic commercialization – the French toy trade has always put more emphasis on the luxury side of the trade, as opposed to mass production, just as French clothes get their name from the exquisite finish and design of their great dress houses, rather than the cheerful appeal of their *prêt à porter* clothes.

In earlier centuries Europe turned to Paris for its fashion dolls, which travelled to England and Germany as well as across the Atlantic. This trend was continued in the great Paris doll trade of the nineteenth century, and in one particular district, around the Choiseul passage, there was a whole quarter of Paris dedicated to making fashion clothes for dolls – tiny hat-makers, shoe-makers, in fact everything in

243 A model of a McCormick-Deering Combine. As the American toy industry developed, it began to cater for every taste from dolls to mechanical toys

miniature, a sort of Lilliputian fashion trade. These artisans still flourish today, and although their quarters have moved, an exquisite doll for a member of a royal family or the little princess of a Sheikh's family, is still to be found in Paris. It was not surprising that in 1938 when the Queen went to Paris the presents given to her for her little daughters, then Princesses Elizabeth and Margaret Rose, were two exquisite dolls. Dolls are still an important French export in the 1960s – and figures show that their export of dolls to other European countries is on the increase.

In the nineteenth century the French showed enormous interest in optical toys, which accorded no doubt with the natural scientific and rational bent of the French mind. The French Panoptique or Magic Lantern made the Magic Lantern highly popular in France, and a great many of them were produced. The French also produced a great many mechanized toys from the 1870s onwards, the use of vulcanized rubber being very popular in their cheap toys.

The famous Parisian toy shop *Au Nain Bleu* (whose luxurious and prettily arranged windows in the Rue Saint-Honoré make one's heart miss a beat, because they seem to epitomize all that is ephemeral yet beautiful about childhood toys) was founded in 1836, showing that throughout the nineteenth century not only toys but toy shops played a part in Parisian toy life. The founder was Jean-Baptiste Chauvière, and his son Edouard Chauvière, installed the shop at 24 boulevard des Capucines, in the place of a shop then called *La Samaritaine*; in 1912 the shop, then run by M. and Mme Fauvet the daughter and son-in-law of M. Chauvière, moved to its present site in the Rue Saint-Honoré. Over fifty years later Mme Fauvet is still at the head of the firm. She is also President of the *Chambre Syndicale nationale des Détaillants en Jeux et Jouets*, and a noted figure in the French toy world. The most elegant toyshop in France has followed the tradition of family ownership for five generations. A modern *Au Nain Bleu* catalogue has four pages of trains, two pages of constructional toys from ancient sailing ships to coronation coaches, a double spread of scientific toys including 'le petit biologiste', 'Poste radio à construire' and 'Astrophone' and then naturally some wonderful dolls' pages.

One is reminded of the success story of the F.A.O. Schwarz toyshop in New York. The founder of this famous shop came to America from Westphalia, and set up his business in 1862. He used to travel to the Leipzig Spring Fair every year to make his selections; his success was largely due to his enterprising catalogues and advertisements.

The rise of the British toy industry follows rather the same pattern as that of America. By the end of the nineteenth century the English toy industry began to make some headway against German predominance. In the 80s William Britain put some toy soldiers on to the market in competition with the continental range, which may have been regarded as a hopeful trend for the British market. The first quality steam locomotive was made in 1901 by Bassett-Lowke. W.J.Bassett-Lowke & Co. was established in the 1890s and while a great deal of equipment was manufactured in England from the start, Bassett-Lowke also made arrangements with the German firm Bing, Carette and Maerklin to manufacture a number of special British type locomotives for them. This continued up to the First World War and was resumed with Bing and Maerklin to some extent in the 1920s.

Games and Toys under H. Richard Simmons, who in 1964 still edits it with his son, was first published in June 1914. May 1915 was the date of the first British Industries Fair – which shows that despite the war business still flourished – and the number of toy exhibits apparently exceeded all others. Indeed a number of toy firms started up in England at this period, as German toys could no longer come

244 Dog Toby, made in Britain by Dean's Rag Book Company. An example of the soft indestructible toy which became so popular from the 1900s onwards

245 A glide-about toy of a duck on wheels being assembled at the Galt Factory. Pull-along toys, ever popular, have been traced as far back as the early Egyptians

246 A toy modelled on a popular make of sports car today. The spoked wheels and bumpers are chromium plated, the engine a replica of the real thing—no detail is overlooked

to Britain, although many firms born in the 1914 war died in the hard economic atmosphere of the 20s.

The history of the British toy firm the Chad Valley Company is a typical example. In 1897 on the outskirts of Birmingham in the valley of the Chad river, Joseph Johnson set up a modern factory for the production of cardboard games. Nowadays, although the Chad Valley group extends over seven factories, the headquarters still occupy the Harborne valley site. The present vice-chairman of the group is Mr Roger Swinburne-Johnson, great grandson of its founder – another instance of the family tradition in the toy business. The Chad Valley group, now producing toys, puppets, plastic and metal items, has always had its eye on promotional items – for example in the 20s, when Bonzo the G.E. Studdy dog was at the height of its fame, Mr Swinburn-Johnson's father hired a dwarf dressed in a Bonzo suit to clown on the Chad Valley stand, to amuse the royal visitors George V and Queen Mary, an example of the popularity of mascot toys during this period.

The toyshops of the Lowther Arcade, and also the specialist shops which sold sheets for toy theatres, were a formative part of the toy world of nineteenth-century England. But no account of the rise of the English toy industry would be complete without a mention of the great London toyshops like Hamleys, and toy departments of big stores, like Selfridges and Gamages, which have acted as entrepots, as Nuremberg did to the German toy trade in days gone by.

The Board of Trade production figures for the United Kingdom up to the end of January 1964 showed a total increase of £2,500,000 in the manufacture of British toys compared with the preceding twelve months. Over £1,500,000 of this is accounted for by the increase in exports, and the main contributors to the increase are metal toys, plastic toys and soft toys – which shows that the British toy business is solid and expanding.

The Russian industry, which like the German industry lies rooted in home-carved wooden figures exported to all parts of Europe, has like the German industry, developed from its folk origins into a well-organized commercial business. There are now toymaking co-operatives and factories making miniature soldiers, whereas the pre-Revolution commercial output had been of poor quality and gaudily painted. At the Leipzig Fair of 1957, steel-helmeted Russian troops with their equipment were exhibited. It is interesting to note that with typical efficiency, some Russian aircraft factories are employed during the slack season making toys to occupy the workers.

The general ability of the toy trade to adapt itself to circumstances seems to be a feature of its existence. The Japanese toy trade has been through a number of phases – it too was rooted in the past with the ancient Japanese toys discussed earlier. It later went through a period when its plentiful cheap labour allowed it to flood European markets with cheap shoddy toys, giving it a bad name, to which the markets of the countries concerned responded by producing toys of quality, if at a higher price. Nowadays both in Japan and Hong Kong toys are being produced where ingenuity is stressed more than quick shoddiness, and in particular the battery toys of Hong Kong seem to show a useful trend in moving toys. There has been a great increase in the export of Japanese dolls to African markets, as these new countries have developed their trading possibilities. Toys are enormously important as an industry to Japan, leading the field in sundry exports by a clear margin of a million dollars, and accounting for a total of nearly 10 million dollars. One cannot help hoping therefore that quality and safety, as well as speedy mass production, will be borne in mind in the making of these toys.

An interesting sidelight on the development of toys as an industry is the enormous importance of Christmas. It is indeed fascinating to see the influence which Christmas has exerted. In an earlier chapter we noticed the part played by the Christmas crèche in the development of toys. But the festival itself began to provide an enormous stimulus. In Puritan America Christmas was actually regarded as a Bacchanalian feast, in which children were not allowed to take part, and Massachusetts laws, which forbade bowling, shuffleboard, mixed dancing and card playing, also forbade observing Christmas. But gradually during the nineteenth century, Christmas began to assume more importance – by 1850 advertisements in newspapers for toys for presents show that Christmas was observed as a time for exchanging gifts. In Europe the feast of St Nicholas (the saint who was supposed to bring a toy to each child) was correspondingly encouraged by manufacturers and toyshops.

The present writer, noting the enormous influence of Christmas in the development of the toy industry, cannot help seeing some connection between the early influence of Christmas in the development of the crèche, and the late nineteenth century and twentieth-century influence of Christmas in the rise of the toy industry.

'The over commercialization of Christmas' is now a commonplace of contemporary discussion, and jokes about the length of the Christmas shopping season fill the newspapers as predictably as the shopping season itself fills the towns. But is it really fair to blame the advertisers and manufacturers so stringently for this trend? If the toy industry is really angled towards the child's needs (as one should hope) it is surely no bad thing that in an affluent society, every child should receive a toy at Christmas. Therefore, insofar as Christmas has been the master, not the tool of the toy trade, one can applaud its influence. It is only the worst excesses of commercialization which appear to contaminate the Feast itself, as well as the public, and here one hopes that the public's own taste will be its best protection.

247 The method which was used to make toys in Saxony 100 years ago. Sections of the spruce trunk are first turned on a lathe to the shape required, then sawn, finished by hand and painted

13 Toys in the Twenties and Thirties

It is hardly surprising that the first impulse of the toy world in the twenties was to revolt against war toys. William Britain's firm, whose toy soldiers have already been discussed, literally turned their swords into ploughshares, and began to produce more peaceable objects such as animals and workers and vehicles, and later a hunt, zoo and circus series. However in the 30s, as armament became increasingly necessary again, so anti-aircraft guns and searchlights and barrage balloons and military vehicles were once again produced from their factories.

But the most interesting development during the inter-war years was surely something rather different. We have seen how the rise of the toy industries transformed toys with modern methods, made them cheaper and brought them within everybody's reach – an excellent and worthwhile trend. But once everybody was able to afford toys, a new question began to be asked – what sort of toy do we want our child to have? This question was obviously not asked for the first time in the thirties, and indeed we have seen how Maria Edgeworth was considering it as early as 1812. The influences which lead to greater theorization about the function and design of toys had their roots in the nineteenth century. In 1904 an article in *Playthings* commented on the fact that the teachers were now exerting an important influence on the toy industry, and enormous attention was being paid to what teachers and grown-ups thought would be good for children. Its editorial runs: 'The kindergarten idea is taking strong hold of the manufacturers of domestic toys . . . any toy which combines a spate of education with a whole lot of pleasure and fun is likely to prove popular.'

The two most important contributors to this development were a man and a woman, Ernest Froebel in Germany and Maria Montessori in Italy. Froebel was an architect who was probably the first person to emphasize the importance of communal life in infant upbringing. His theory of the Kindergarten began in 1837 when he opened one at Keilhau near Blankenburg. Here he elaborated a series of toys known as 'Occupations' which included balls, blocks for buildings, coloured tablets for designs and coloured papers to cut and fold. The Kindergarten found ready acceptance in nineteenth-century England, and Muirhead Mitchell, Inspector of Church Schools in the Eastern counties, recommended Kindergarten methods in 1854, especially the use of toys by teachers. He wrote:

'A set of playthings, cups and saucers, a small kitchen with its implements really modelled on life, a butcher's shop, a drawing-room and parlour . . . I believe that the bulk of education and happiness of the younger classes will be materially enhanced if grants of pictures and toys were made by the Committee of Council to infant schools.'

The 1870s were times of rapid expansion of Kindergarten ideas both in America and Germany. The essence of Froebel's teaching was 'Never, if you can help it, deprive the child of the sacred right of discovery', or in short 'Learn by doing'.

The mainspring of Maria Montessori's work was rather different – she did not believe, as some critics suggested, in letting children do as they liked, but relied

248 Mickey Mouse. This toy, based on the Walt Disney cartoon character, leapt to fame in 1934 and has since become a classic

249 Dr Maria Montessori based her teaching methods on children's spontaneous interest in their work: here she is shown visiting in November 1946 a Montessori School in Acton – a borough where her methods were used extensively

on their spontaneous interest in their work. Noting in children a love of order and a love of repetition, and the fact that they prefer to work rather than play, she encouraged these tendencies. Some of Dr Montessori's friends, society ladies in Rome who were interested in her work with poor children provided her with costly toys, elegant dolls, dolls' houses, dolls' crockery and even a dolls' kitchen. But she noticed that the children never chose these toys, in spite of her special efforts to show them how to play with them. Dr Montessori concluded that the need of children is work rather than play. She wrote: 'I set to work like a peasant woman who having set aside a good store of seed-corn has found a fertile field in which she may freely sow it. I was wrong. I had hardly turned over the clods of my field when I found gold instead of wheat; the clod had concealed a precious treasure.' This treasure to which she referred was the normal characteristics of childhood which had previously gone unrevealed. Dr Montessori founded her schools on the spontaneous self-discipline of children when happily occupied, and as a result of an LCC investigation in 1918 Montessori methods were imported to England.

Thus by the twenties we find alongside the bright multitude of toys in the shops,

250 *Paul and Marjorie Abbatt believed passionately that toys were not merely expensive breakable extras for children of the rich but an essential part of every child's development. 'The first train' meets their requirements with its simple, solid and well-made structure*

a new trend for plain toys, which also had an educational function. These toys filled the new nursery schools. They also filled the shops, and it is to the credit of manufacturers that they recognized and filled the needs of the kindergartens, in spite of the slower recognition of the public for what was best, if not brightest, for their children. In the United States the Playskool Manufacturing Company was founded in 1928 to fill these needs, and the hammer, nail and peg table, a typical product, were patented in the same year.

In England a remarkable shop was opened by the combined efforts of two school teachers Paul and Marjorie Abbatt. While on their honeymoon in Vienna Mr and Mrs Abbatt read the works of Susan Isaacs, in which she pointed out that toys were not merely expensive breakable extras on the floor of a rich child's nursery, but an essential part of every child's development. Susan Isaacs had gathered material for her books from her work at the Malting House School for young children at Cambridge from 1924 to 1927. She had answered an advertisement for this experimental school put in the *New Statesman and Nation* by Geoffrey N. Pyke, owner of the school, who wanted a head teacher who would really explore the development of

251 Bricks typical of the plain lines, solid materials and bright colours which people sought to put before children in the thirties

children. A very free atmosphere was introduced at the school with play material to test the children's development, as a result of which Susan Isaacs drew a number of conclusions which impressed the Abbatts. In particular Susan Isaacs established that understanding grows best from immediate experience, and she provided the children with all sorts of stimuli like see-saws, hooks and weights, sewing rooms with stuffs, and weaving machines, which were a far cry from the toys then in the shops.

In Vienna, the Abbatts collected such toys as Susan Isaacs recommended. They also visited Kindergartens there and were very impressed with what they saw, for example solid little brooms being used for real work by children, instead of tiny breakable ones. They brought these toys home and had an exhibition of them in their own flat, including some other similar toys from America, and as in the course of the exhibition all their friends wanted to buy the toys, they decided to open a shop. The first catalogue was illustrated with drawings by John Skeaping. The lease of their first shop in Tavistock Square, however, did not permit them to buy and sell, and every toy had to be posted, which involved tremendous labour, so that eventually a move was made to the present premises in Wigmore Street. Their subsequent history has proved the immense appeal of their simple good toys. Even during the war, supplies would somehow be obtained, often from advertisements of oddments for sale by the Ministry of Supply – the sacks would be sorted through eagerly to find something suitable; from this sprang one of their most popular toys, the idea of buying a bag of 'oddments'. The Abbatts did particularly well after the war with schools, as the idea of play-in-school spread from nursery school to infants from 5–7. Of course some of their earliest toys were originally American like the famous post-box (figure 255) and the first train (figure 250). Many people who grew up in the thirties must recall the famous Abbatt climbing frame (figure 254) with a nostalgic and grateful feeling for this durable miniature repository of adventure and make-believe. The climbing frame enjoyed by the present writer and her seven brothers and sisters is now enjoyed by her own family of five – a striking testimonial to the unbreakability of this particular type of plain toy.

The dolls' house of the thirties is a typical example of the new trend; house and furniture are for the first time planned to be strong, as opposed to beautiful or

252 On preceding page *The dining-room from Queen Mary's dolls' house. The most eminent craftsmen and artists of the day were employed to make the miniatures for this house*
Opposite *The elaborate façade of the dolls' house*
Right *An elevation showing the Queen's bedroom, bathroom and wardrobe*

desirable. Hands are supposed to have easy access to the interior of the dolls' house, and thus doors are thought to be unnecessary. The Abbatt dolls' house was described in the catalogue as 'simple, so it lends itself to many play uses i.e. house, farm, garage, shop'. In fact it consisted of three wooden units of sitting-room, kitchen, and bedroom, all of which could be switched round. How different from the elaborate and fragile dolls' house of the nineteenth century.

The first Abbatt catalogue had a short foreword, which was the forerunner of the elaborate text which precedes the present catalogue, and gives clues to the types of toys enjoyed by children of all different ages. It read: 'We have made it our serious endeavour to set out the 25 best toys for each age.' This catalogue, which exists in very much the same form at the present day, was obviously a boon to parents, and represented a completely new departure in toy buying from the idea of the father rushing into the shop and buying the most expensive toy, or merely the one he would most like to play with. The present Abbatt catalogue contains this apologia: 'The toys we recommend are not any special sort, but ordinary toys made stronger and better than usual and chosen correctly for the age of the child. . . . Toys to match the vitality of childhood. Children will use them upside down and the opposite way from that intended. But whichever way up, and however used, the toy must not break, nor fail the child.' The Abbatts also add: 'A child can be swamped by toys. Do not give too many. He will benefit from one toy more than from two at any one time, from a few more than a many. They are not trivialities . . . they are the tools of his development.'

This is obviously a very different attitude from that of the slogan-happy advertisers in the toy market, and it might therefore be fair to say that from the twenties onwards toys as a whole divide into two streams: those giving first priority to

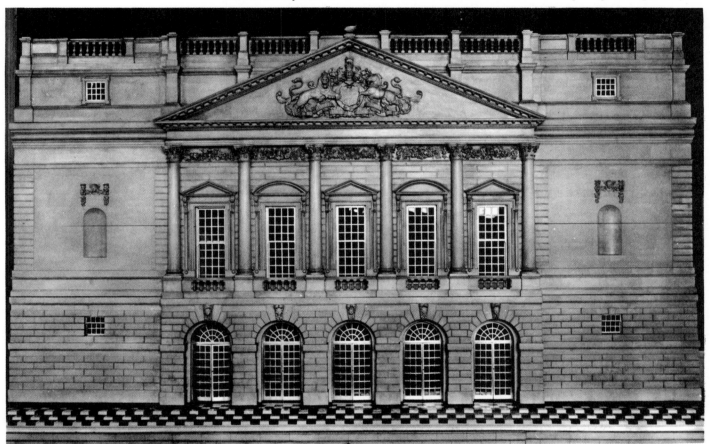

the child's development, and those belonging to the brighter if more garish and less psychologically sound world of commercial toy production.

But the trend towards the 'good toy' was not the only trend in the thirties. There are beautiful dolls dating from the thirties, which are truly artistic efforts, to be compared with the exquisite antique dolls of earlier periods. Queen Mary's dolls house, for example, made in 1924 (figure 252), represented a serious attempt to reproduce exactly the life of the time, and can be regarded more as sociological commentary than an actual toy. The late Princess Marie-Louise knew that Queen Mary had a great tendresse for objects d'art: consequently she decided to ask Sir Edwin Lutyens to design a doll's house worthy of presentation to Queen Mary by a group of wellwishers and friends. Lutyens was at the time engaged on the large scale task of building the city of New Delhi, and the contrast between the contract for the huge city and the tiny dolls' house appealed to him. Lutyens then decided that the miniature house should be decorated with pictures and furniture specifically made to scale by the leading painters and craftsmen of the day, so that, when finished, it would enable future generations to see how a king and queen of

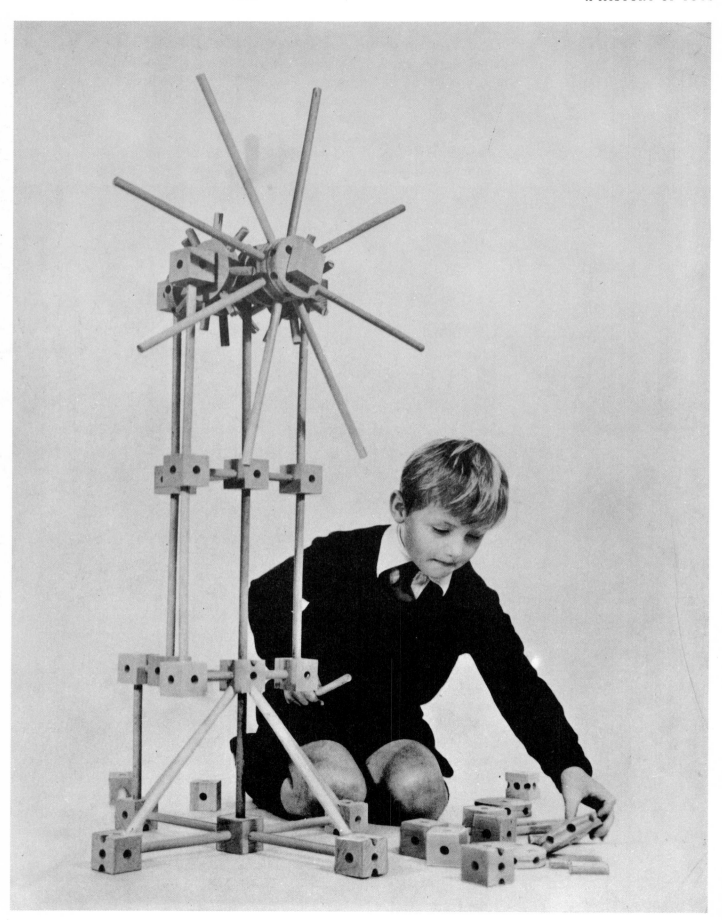

253 Left *A constructional toy, allowing a child's natural desire to build and create to find an outlet in his playthings*

254 The climbing frame: children are able to put this toy to many imaginative uses, such as making houses, as well as actually climbing on it

255 The posting box, one of the first toys which enable children to use their own initiative

England lived in the twentieth century and what authors, artists and craftsmen of note there were during their reign.

Queen Mary herself approved this evidence of historic purpose in her dolls' house, which was also to provide a microcosm of her own taste. She took great interest in the planning and furnishing of the house and all the various details of it – the gold plate, the books written by contemporary authors in their own hands in the King's Library, the bathrooms with their floors of African marble and mother-of-pearl, with real water spurting from the taps, and the gramophone in the nursery which played *God Save the King*. In the garage below the dolls' house were extremely costly reproductions of the royal Daimlers. In the cellar, moreover, were bottles with real wine – a fact which caused some offence to the teetotallers among the King's subjects. Mr James Pope-Hennessey, Queen Mary's biographer, has described it as 'eerily empty' – 'Nothing, in fact, went on inside the Queen's dolls' house, for it lacked an essential component: a family of doll royalty. . . . By the green garden door a miniature white dog waited "expectantly . . . till it shall please the Queen, his mistress, to walk in her garden".' However, since the dolls' house was not intended to be a toy, one can surely applaud the exquisite craftsmanship, and regard it as being in the tradition of the luxurious Dutch cabinets of the seventeenth century, meant to be admired not played with.

But the thirties were not only a period of ideas and craftsmanship, they were also a time when new materials were of considerable importance. Charles S. Raizen of Transogram, recalls how by a strange chance in America the depression years of the 30s were of great significance to manufacturers, because they were able to break away from the manufacture of toys out of scrap materials. 'Auto scrap had been our raw material for steel toys; dolls' dresses were made from the cutaway of the ladies garment manufacturer, wooden toys from the off-fall of the lumber mill. For the first time we were able to buy prime material of high quality. Lumber mills, steel mills, textile mills were desperately looking for business during those depression years and they were happy to find new customers in the growing toy manufacture.' Toy manufacturers were able to hire skilled labourers, who were now willing to work for the rates of pay which toy manufacturers could afford.

The use of rubber, later plastic, and still later vinyl in making dolls' faces gave

them much greater verisimilitude, and the American Trade Association gives the doll's face in its more lifelike representations in America as a typical example of the development of the American toy industry in the twentieth century. The psychologists thoroughly approved of rubber, which seemed ideally suited to reproduce a human baby in as lifelike a manner as possible – rubber dolls were perfect for bathing, feeding and nappy-changing – all the natural functions of a mother towards her baby. Celluloid also enjoyed popularity, witness the Kewpie dolls mentioned in an earlier chapter, but rag, stockinet and other softer materials were more thoroughly approved of, because they did not have the dangers inherent in celluloid. At an earlier date a famous series of rag dolls were those made by Martha Chase, creator of 'Chase stockinet dolls' and founder of the Chase doll factory.

Two interesting fabric toy makers in Europe in the 20s and 30s were Madame Lenci in Italy and Frau Kathe Kruse in Germany. The Lenci dolls are highly prized by collectors of the more modern type of doll for their excellence and Madame Lenci made many charming types of dolls of which, in the opinions of experts, the best were her child dolls. The hallmark of a Lenci doll was the prettiness and

257 The animal has taken many different toy shapes in history – in our own century, it is found mainly in the shape of the soft toy

258 From the Catalogue of Dean's Hygienic Dolls, Toys, Plush Animals, Rag Books *1935. (a) Nightdress cases : Marina, Yvonne and Olga (b) Dismal and Cheerful Desmond. The nightdress case – the toy put to a practical purpose – and the mascot toy, are both typical trends of the thirties*

good taste of their clothing, Mme Lenci having begun life as an artist. Mme Lenci died in 1951, but her factory, which closed during the Second World War, has now been reopened. Frau Kruse made a series of baby or toddler dolls in pre-war Germany; her factory also ceased production during the Second World War, when it fell under the displeasure of Hitler, but Frau Kruse is still alive and has now reopened it herself.

Soft toys enjoyed enormous popularity in the 30s and fitted in well with the continued popularity of mascot toys. Chad Valley enjoyed terrific success with their Felix the Cat character toys, and later made Pip Squeak and Wilfred toys, based on the strip cartoons, and Mabel Lucie Attwell doll-toys. All this was before the Mickey Mouse boom in 1934. They developed their export trade strongly at this time, and it is amusing to find that Ludo was much in demand in West Africa as an adult gambling game.

Another famous name in British toys, the Dean's Rag Book Company, sold a great number of its soft toys of the 20s and 30s, having been originally founded in 1903 by a gentleman who envisaged a really indestructible book for children on the grounds that children – in his own words 'wear their food and eat their clothes'. Their rag books enjoyed and still enjoy enormous success all over the world. During the First World War editions were actually produced with Russian texts, but unfortunately they never reached their destined market as the Germans marched into Vilna the day after the shipment had arrived, and its ulitimate fate is unknown. Incidentally not all of the rag books were used for their correct purpose – the natives in the Gold Coast wear shorts made up from the rag book waste sheets, an interesting example of utility playthings. The Dean

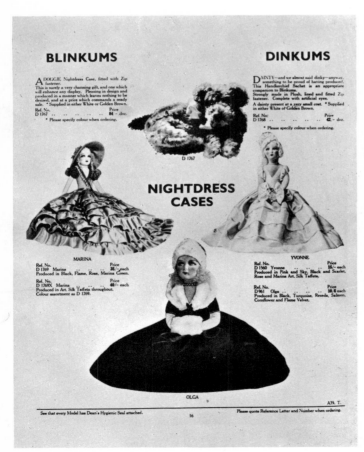

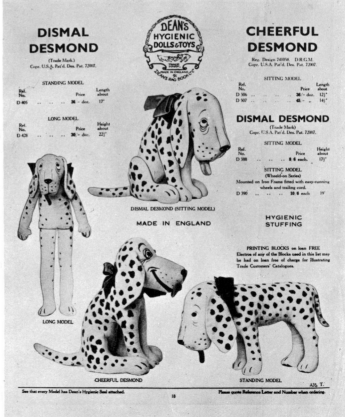

259 A rabbit warren filled with miniature rabbits, made by Yootha Rose

Rag Book Company's soft toys, are also immensely characteristic of their period; a 1928 catalogue includes Willow pattern dolls; Posy Buds ('produced in response to numerous requests for a felt-dressed doll'); Smart set dolls ('Dolls that nice children would like to play with'); Princess dolls ('as purchased by HRH Princess Mary'); Tatters – the Hospital pup (his paw is bandaged); Dismal Desmond, Jolly Jumbo, Bunnikins, and a series of other velvet toys, which have a special period charm. Their 1935 Marina doll nightcase – presumably based on the enormous popularity of the wedding of the late Duke of Kent and Princess Marina – is redolent of the taste of the time, as are a series of other mascots and dolls (figure 258) called Precious, Dimple, Nero the News Hound (well known to readers of the Daily Mirror) and even an extraordinary striped rabbit rejoicing in the name of Belisha Beaconey. Obviously in an age when a Belisha Beacon was a novelty it was unnecessary to do more than present this mascot 'with rolling eyes – "green eyes" which signal a clear road to success'. The catalogues of the toy manufacturers of this period provide valuable material for the social historian, while the ordinary observer is seized by nostalgia for these forgotten favourites.

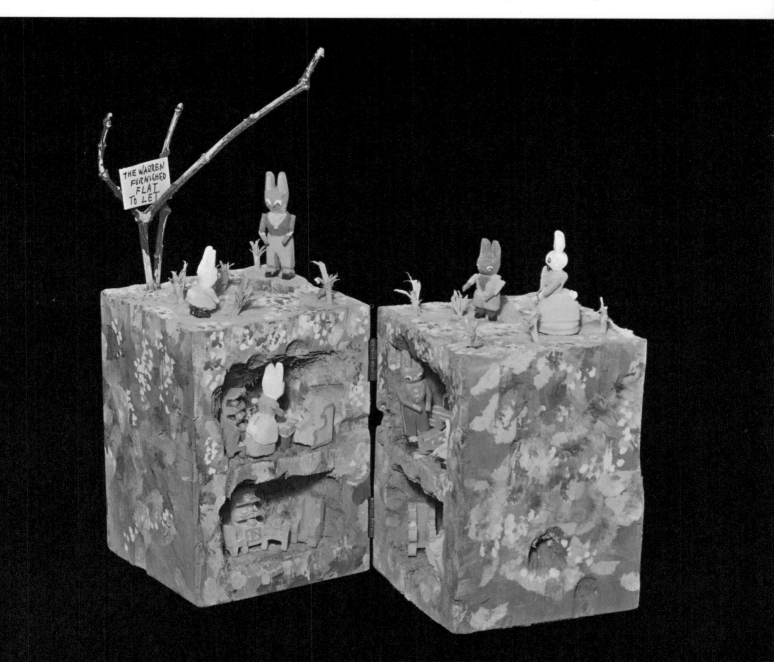

14 Modern Trends

One of the most interesting modern trends in toys is the continued popularity of the Wild West. Perhaps some parents consider a tomahawk less deadly than a gun, and think that they have discovered a natural outlet for the aggressiveness of their children in games of cowboys and Indians which are less disturbing than battles between modern soldiers. A psychiatrist wrote recently in *Toys International* along these lines: 'We need our cowboys and Indians, our cops and robbers. There has been from time to time a tendency to deprecate the violence, inherent in so much children's play – the eternal "bang you're dead" type of thing. But humans are naturally aggressive and it is through aggressive play that we learn to use and control it.'

Psychology apart, why did the Wild West take such a strong hold on the imagination of children, so that wigwams, tomahawks and Indian headdresses became an essential part of childhood? It is probably because the period when the modern toy industry developed on a large scale coincided with the decade which gave rise to the legends of the Wild West. Although the actual frontier phase runs from 1850 to 1900, the decade when the legends were popularized was 1870 to 1880. The arrival of the budget mass appeal toy came at a time when Western events were front page news the world over. The cowboy and Indian set (figure 261) was conceivably the first democratic toy – because the Western background was a fantasy for all European children – appealing equally to all income groups, and opening up new fields for the toy trade.

There has been a continuous development of this market: nowadays children want rather stylized, gaudy clothes, not identified too closely with any one character like Davy Crockett of Wyatt Earp. The working kit in the old West was in fact unattractive, and present day suits are actually modelled on what the Western heroes wore at rodeos. Modern manufacturers of Indian sets take great trouble to make the totems on their wigwams accurate, and they show the true totem patterns of various tribes, just as tartans have to be accurate on Scottish toys.

A more peaceful trend in Indian toys has been noticed by one manufacturer. There appears to be an increased demand not only for the wigwam, but also for the Indian squaw's cooking utensils, as well as the traditional bow and arrow. Is this an example of peace rearing its head, now that cooking pots and fires are being included in the sets: or is it perhaps an indication of co-educational trends – little boys are now allowing their sisters to join in the play.

The firearm also has a continuous appeal, and here the nature of the war toy is more evident than in the straightforward Indian set. Lone Star Products produce a series of realistic guns called Frontier Scout, Sharpshooter, Cobra and Ringo Ricochet – these are four from a full range of die-cast metal pistols and rifles. There are great attempts at accuracy, comparable to Britain's efforts to make their soldiers realistic, and Lone Star have even set up a museum of weapons to provide reference material, proving the fantastic pains to which toy manufacturers are

260 A modern copy of an Indian headdress: children's natural aggressiveness coupled with the current interest and heroic imagery of the Wild West gave rise to the game of cowboys and Indians.

261 Right *A stylized and gaudy cowboy outfit typical of the play suits young boys wear today*

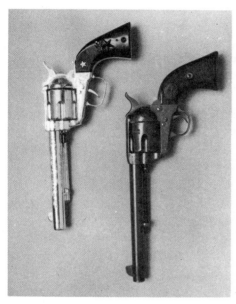

262 Above *An 1875 'Peacemaker' 45 calibre gun* (right) *with a toy gun* (left) *showing the care taken by manufacturers to model their guns on the real thing*

263 *The James Bond cult has produced the 007 pistol complete with detachable silencer*

264 *A modern peepshow depicting the coronation of Queen Elizabeth II in Westminster Abbey, made by Edwin Smith*

265 *Bullock cart of terra cotta from Portugal shown with a group of wooden dolls designed by the Portuguese artist Tom*

266 A collection of contemporary dolls from Holland, formed by friends of the owner in the Netherlands Diplomatic Service, who sent figures from all over the world. The average height of each figure is three inches

prepared to go. But Mr Perrin, director of Lone Star, points out that in a genuine toy: 'The gun mechanism and its appearance should be simple. Indeed, once again, an essential which applies to the value of any toy, not just Western gear; that it should stimulate rather than stultify its owner's imagination, providing the one tenth original idea round which the child can develop his private fantasy.'

The present writer feels that children are better off provided with safe guns, to drain off their natural aggressiveness, than sheltered from things which will soon be apparent to them in the world around. At the same time one feels a natural sympathy for the parent who wants at any cost to bring up a peace-loving, peace-promoting child, and wonders whether giving it a gun is the best method! It is inevitable that an age which has known wars should produce soldiers and war-toys. Some of these are more openly warlike in nature – for example GI Joe, produced by Hassenfeld Brothers in America (figure 267) described as 'Americas's movable fighting man', and including action soldier, action marine, action sailor, and action pilot. GI Joe's Beach Head Field pack set is advertised 'with ML rifle plus hand grenades. Cartridge belt fits GI Joe and has pockets that snap open. Set

267 A modernized version of an old theme, G.I. Joe reflects the persisting popularity of martial toys with children – and toy manufacturers

features field pack plus entrenching tool with cover.' This is obviously the natural development of an age when a child's admired father is dressed up as GI Joe. As long as men go to war and armies exist children will want to play with soldiers, and therefore one can scarcely blame the manufacturers for trying to fill the need. At the same time on the principle of the chicken and the egg, it might be argued that as long as the children are given soldiers to play with, they themselves will grow up prepared to be soldiers – but here the argument begins to extend far outside the realm of a history of toys.

268 1/500th scale model of H.M.S. Exeter made from a plastic construction kit by Revell Authentic Kits Inc. Innumerable plastic models have been available from the fifties onwards. The advent of plastic answered many problems : here was a cheap substance which could be accurately cast and was, with the aid of quick drying glue, easy to assemble

For those who believe that small boys will inevitably turn their toys into instruments of war, whatever the good intentions of their parents, Saki (H.H.Munro) provides an ironic commentary on the subject in his story *The Toys of Peace.* Published in 1919, it was inspired by an actual newspaper cutting from a London paper in March 1914 which read as follows: 'In the view of the National Peace Council, there are grave objections to presenting our boys with regiments of fighting men, batteries of guns, and squadrons of *Dreadnoughts.* . . . At the Children's Welfare Exhibition, the Peace Council will make an alternative suggestion to parents in the shape of an exhibition of "peace toys". In front of a specially-painted representation of the Peace Palace at the Hague will be grouped, not miniature soldiers but miniature civilians, not guns but ploughs and the tools of industry.' Fired by this message, the well-intentioned parents of the story provide their boys with a new line in 'peace toys', which include miniature lead figures of notables such as John Stuart Mill, the poetess Mrs Hemans, the astronomer Sir John Herschel, as well as other anonymous worthies such as sanitary inspectors, district councillors and the like. The only building provided is not a fort but a model of the Manchester branch of the Young Women's Christian Association.

269 A Revell construction kit of a Mercury capsule and Atlas booster, appealing to the natural interest of the modern child in space flight

Alas for the 'peace toys'! The children greet them blankly and ask *how* exactly they are to play with them. An uncle brightly suggests a General Election, at which the children exclaim:

' "With rotten eggs, and free fights, and ever so many broken heads!" . . . "And noses all bleeding and everybody drunk as can be" ' echoed Bertie, who had carefully studied one of Hogarth's pictures. Naturally the grown-ups discourage this, as being back to the bad old days. But by the end of the story, the children have of course been surprised with the district councillors and sanitary inspectors drawn

270 Overleaf *Battery and key-wound robots inspired by T.V. serials and the machine age. Some of these robots talk, gnash their teeth or, like the one on the right, come with an attacking kit of guns and suction darts, flashing bright coloured lights. These weird creatures are great favourites with children*

271 Lego in operation. *Invented in Denmark by Papa Christiansen, Lego provides infinite possibilities for a child to develop and satisfy his creative and constructive instincts*

272 *A plastic version of the metal Meccano set patented by Frank Hornby in 1901. After watching a crane at work, it occurred to Hornby that models could easily be made out of a small number of simple parts. The Meccano set, first called Mechanics Made Easy, provides an ideal outlet for mechanically minded boys*

273 Opposite *A constructional toy for the very young: these acrobats can be arranged in a variety of ways*

up in battle array, under the command of John Stuart Mill, now transformed by red ink into Marshal Saxe. Robert Raikes is Louis XIV, and even Mrs Hemans has been made into Madame de Maintenon. The children blandly explain the plot:

'Louis orders his troops to surround the Young Women's Christian Association and seize the lot of them. "Once back at the Louvre and the girls are mine" he exclaims. We must use Mrs Hemans again for one of the girls. She says "Never," and stabs Marshal Saxe to the heart.'

Saki's parents creep away, disillusioned at the total failure of their experiment, and the children revert to playing with ordinary soldiers.

Less controversial are space toys (figure 269), which are the natural reflections of our space age, and one is not surprised to find Christmas catalogues filled with rockets and rocketry, which gratify an early bent for science in much the same way as did the nineteenth-century optical toys. So-called nuclear toys, like nuclear submarines, tend to be almost identical with the submarines of one's childhood, with the word nuclear happily inserted into the text – proving that much as children like novelty in approach, their basic need for a toy to float in the bath or pond or river has remained the same for thousands of years.

Constructional toys are a great modern boon: during the last war aircraft constructional kits rose to heights of popularity. The present trend, according to one leading manufacturer of kits, is for simpler toys. Certainly a system such as Lego (figure 271), is rightly advertised as 'more than an amusing toy and hobby, it is also an enthrallingly interesting and instructive game' and it has immense adult appeal as well as to children – an example of the co-operative toy with which adults and children can play happily together.

Lego, from the Danish word 'Leg' to play, was the brain child of Papa Christiansen in Denmark, a poor man with four sons, who made wooden toys during the depression of the early 30s to amuse his children, and later took his toys to a neighbouring farmer to barter them for food. When times improved, he became a full time toymaker. It was his son Gottfried who turned first from wooden bricks to plastic, and then to interlocking bricks, so that the plastic bricks would not all fall down: thus Lego was born. The Lego factory is still situated in the remote Danish village of Billund, although it employs 600 people. To combat its remoteness an airport has been built, with the runway marked with giant Lego bricks.

275 Opposite *The 'House of Cards', one of several toys invented by the American designer Charles Eames, who has introduced a lively, sophisticated element into toy design*

No consideration of modern toys would be complete without mention of television and its influence. Television heroes and comic animals or cartoons have given rise to a whole new series of mascot toys, and in Christmas catalogues of the sixties it is fascinating to see the numbers of toys which are advertised 'as on television'. Moreover television itself offers an excellent medium for manufacturers to advertise their wares.

Sindy, a doll with a teenager's body and clothes (figure 282), is the evidence of another modern trend – the cultivation of the teenage market. Here the enormous wage packet of the earning teenager has clearly had its influence on the manufacturer. The most famous teenage doll, Barbie, with her 'date' Ken (figure 281), is also enjoyed by younger children although her aims and desires are so clearly those of a teenager. Barbie, according to her promoters, 'Can pose as if running, cheerleading or modelling . . . comes with three glamorous high fashion wigs – bubble-on-bubble, pageboy and sidepart flip.' Barbie's date Ken is a manly 12½ inches 'Dreamy date for Barbie. Ken's manly physique is molded of sturdy plastic . . . That realistic crew cut is molded in and painted . . . Smartly tailored outfits and accessories listed below will make Barbie proud of him on every occasion.' Barbie's outfits are listed as Barbie baby-sits, Friday night date, Career girl, Dinner at 8, Solo in the spot light, Sophisticated lady. Ken's (which scarcely seem to match) are Campus hero, Touchdown, Dream boat and Ski Champion. Accessories follow like Barbie and Ken's Hot Rod, and Barbie's fashion shop, bed and house.

Truly this is a very different world from the elegant passive wax doll of the Montanaris, yet let us not scorn it too much – for if toys and dolls are part of the necessary fantasy of people in the process of growing-up, there is surely no harm in Barbie's own world of fantasy? And if even adults, as we have seen, can join in the world of fantasy through the medium of toys, who knows what happiness and solace the dream world of Barbie and Ken has brought to an unhappy teenager, lacking her own Ken, her own shared Hot Rod. . . .

Modern mascots seem to have a droll and offbeat aspect – the Gonk for example with its innocent appealing moon face, and the good-luck Troll also from Denmark (figure 276), ugly at first glance to the critical adult, but curiously attractive to children, presumably satisfying the taste for the grotesque that we have observed

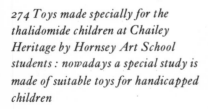

274 *Toys made specially for the thalidomide children at Chailey Heritage by Hornsey Art School students : nowadays a special study is made of suitable toys for handicapped children*

276 *A troll family from Denmark designed by Thomas Dam: the whimsical appearance of trolls appeals to children, and there is also a tradition that they bring good luck.*

throughout history. Less attractive is the trend for weirdies, and even blood stained mummies as toys. A construction kit called 'Make your own Monster' seems rather a fearful extension of the grotesque in toys. As for the Lindy Loonys – described in *British Toys* as the most recent craze in the plastic kit world – one's mind boggles at the thought of the repressions which they are satisfying, when one learns there are four characters in the series – Big Wheeler, Satan's Crate, The Road Hog and Scuttle Bucket. They come in striking boxes with slogans like 'Loathsome but Lovable' and 'Repulsive Genuine Plastic Assembly Kit'. The most popular of the four is reputed to be Scuttle Bucket, which is described as a 'fractured nightmare in a coal scuttle'. Equally chilling is the *Make a Monster* advertised in John Plain of Chicago's Christmas catalogue: 'Make three of the scariest, most spine-tingling monsters ever seen. Kit lets you create $9\frac{1}{2}$ ins tall Frankenstein, $8\frac{1}{2}$ ins tall Dracula, and $9\frac{1}{2}$ ins tall Wolf Man all with your bare hands. Each of these plastic monsters is a scream . . . perfectly detailed down to the last fang.' It needs all one's sense of history, one's memories of the twisting birds of Nuremberg and the guillotine toys of the French Revolution, not to shrink from these apparently

277 *Nina the spy doll, who carried medicines in the crown of her head during the American Civil War*

278 *The spy dolls used to smuggle microfilm out of Austria*

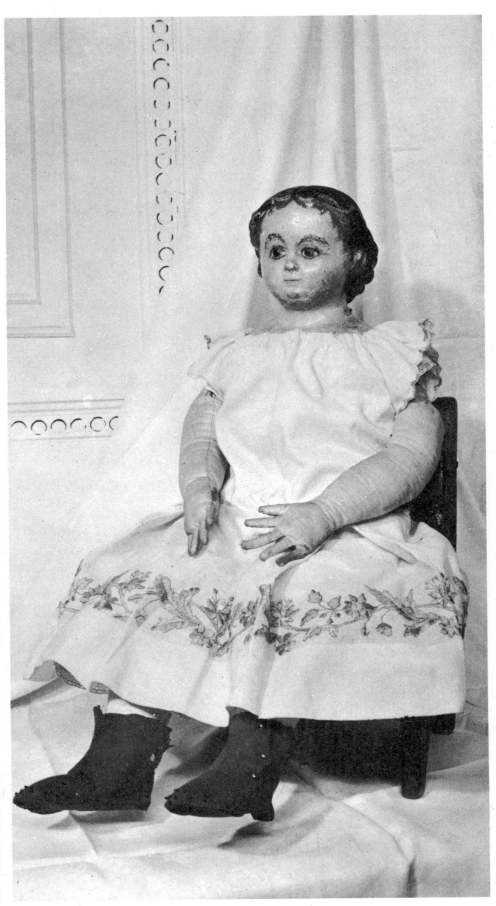

279 *A Rosebud doll, 12 inches high, made by Rosedale Plastics Ltd. Rosebud dolls are famous for their immaculately styled hair and colourful, removable accessories*

280 *Pebbles Flintstone, daughter of the Stone Age cartoon couple Fred and Wilma, from the television series* The Flintstones. *Pebbles is 14-inches high with fully jointed arms and legs and movable tilting head*

horrific modern tendencies, and to remember that they represent only a recurrent phenomenon.

In the world of dolls, as of other toys, the introduction of plastics and vinyl has brought revolutionary changes. Dolls have become much cheaper and more hygienic. Rosebud dolls, for example (figure 279), were the result of a decision by T. Eric Smith, who founded Rosedale Plastics Ltd, to break away from the wooden toys which had been the mainstay of his family business in the past and to concentrate on dolls made by new techniques. The firm, incidentally, was originally less euphoniously called Nene Plastics Ltd. It was always Mr Smith's custom to present young visitors to the factory with a doll as they left, and after one such presentation he asked a little girl what she liked most about her gift. She replied: 'What lovely rosebud lips the doll has!' and so the name was born.

Not every modern doll is as innocent as her wide-eyed stare would suggest. Recently a newspaper headline *Wooden dolls in spy case* was followed by a story of international espionage reminiscent of *The Third Man*. The object of the spy ring concerned was to discover Austrian industrial secrets, in particular those of a metal factory at Plansee near Reutte in the Austrian Tyrol, which produces special alloys of great hardness used for space projects. Microfilm giving details of the alloy was smuggled out of Austria in a series of specially constructed wooden dolls (figure 278). As the following story illustrates, dolls apparently have a sinister connotation in certain circles. Mr Anthony Powell, the English novelist, was asked to a British Council lunch in London in honour of a fellow novelist from behind the Iron Curtain, and told that he had to sit next to the Secret Police man who was reputed to be 'rather difficult' conversationally. This turned out to be all too true, so that he was grateful to discover that the man had two daughters of about four or five. On being asked to another luncheon the next day, he had the happy thought of buying two little dolls for the Secret Police man's daughters, hoping to ensure a further flow of conversation. As luck would have it, when he arrived for lunch, the Secret Police man was already there. Mr Powell produced the dolls with enthusiasm. To his amazement, on hearing the words: 'I bought little presents for Natasha and Maria' his companion went ashen and dashed from the room, presumably to destroy them in his search for microfilm!

The use of dolls for spying is not confined to the present day. Illustrated here is Nina (figure 277), a doll now lodged peacefully in the Confederate Museum at Richmond, Virginia. But Nina is in fact a retired agent enjoying her old age, for she was used during the American Civil War by General Batton Anderson's niece to carry medicines in her hollow head – the medicines concerned were morphine and quinine, and both were declared contraband by the US government. Yet both were vitally needed by the Confederates, morphine for use in the treatment of wounds and amputations, and quinine for the malaria so prevalent in the South at that time.

It is important to acknowledge the enormous therapeutic work which has been done with toys for sick children, crippled children and the mentally deficient. Puppets and marionettes have a valuable place in training deaf children to speak, and gay marionette shows also provide therapy for disturbed children. Recently art students from Hornsey spent a year designing therapeutic toys for thalidomide children in conjunction with the staff at Chailey Heritage, the centre for training thalidomide children in Sussex (figure 274). These included a swing, see-saw, slide, two carts, and a musical box, all adapted to the special needs of these children. The see-saw had sprung ends to help it bounce up again on touching the ground, the carts worked by swaying from side to side, and the musical box was in the form of a

*281 Ken and Barbie, the teenager dolls,
dressed up for an evening out. Both of
them are equipped with a wardrobe of
clothes for every occasion. Although
modelled on teenagers, Ken and Barbie
also appeal to the doll-play instinct in
much younger children*

Sleepy-time   **Shopping-in-the-rain**   **Dream Date**   **Undie-world**

Sweet Swimmer   **Leather Look**   **Out-and-about**   **Sloppy Joe**

282 *A catalogue showing the clothes that can be bought for doll Sindy, the English equivalent of the American Barbie. Like Barbie, Sindy has a boy-friend, Paul, and she also has a little red sports car. The Sindy Club keeps members informed of their activities and latest additions to their wardrobe.*

Country Walk **Pony Club** **Bridesmaid** **Seaside Sweetheart**

Summery Days **Frosty Nights** **Coffee Date** **Sindy's Wardrobe**

283 The rocking-horse which once belonged to the present Prince of Wales.

balloon case – the child blows the balloon up through the tube and then as the air escapes it plays a tune.

Dolls have made a significant contribution to the history of medicine. From the sixteenth to the nineteenth centuries ivory manikins were used for instruction in anatomy, the forerunners of the medical dolls. They usually went in pairs, male and female, and the female was often pregnant. The famous American Chase dolls, made by Martha Chase in the early twentieth century, were frequently used to train nurses before the First World War.

The use of toys with the orthopaedically handicapped and cerebrally palsied, as well as the handicapped and deaf, is now the subject of special study and there exists considerable literature on the subject. Special magnetized toys have now been invented for children who are incapable of picking up an object if it drops to the floor. The needs of blind children have been the subject of careful study – here musical toys and toys permanently attached to some fixed object so that they cannot be lost have been developed. Sock puppets have been used to teach deaf children to open their mouths and make sounds.

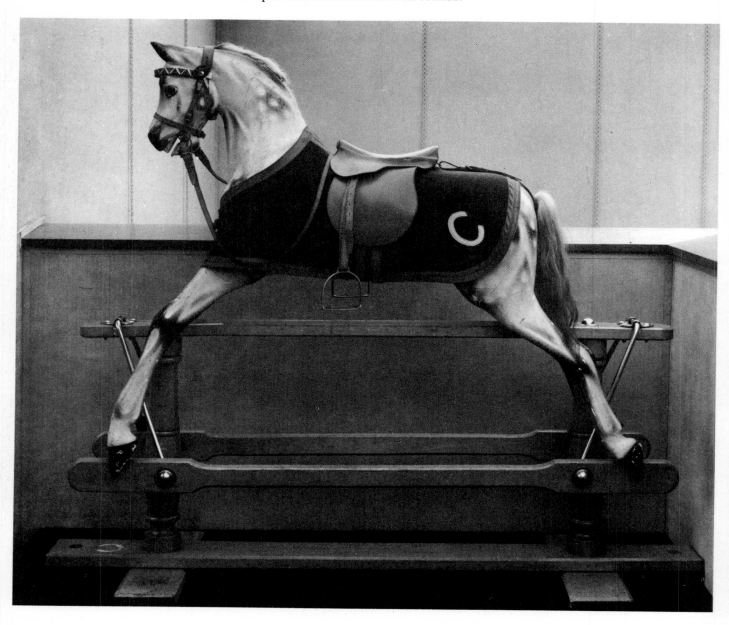

284 *A Triang baby-walker together with bricks and plastic cups and saucers.*

285 *Children happily at play using miniature but sturdy and workable wheelbarrow, spade, crane and buckets*

286 *A collection of modern, hand-made soft and wooden toys*

287 *'Quick Fit' cars by Frog. The parts of these electric motorized cars fit together quickly and easily. The electric motor is started and stopped by moving the front bumper in and out.*

At the same time the safety of existing toys for ordinary children is being widely investigated. The use of paint containing poisonous lead has been the subject of violent protests by parents and responsible bodies, and legislation has been called for on the subject. Toys, like all intimate objects, can carry disease. Lead poisoning was discussed in medical literature as early as the nineteenth century, but still continues. Even syphilis has been known in the past to be passed from toy to toy and children infected. Kites and electric trains can both cause electrocution, the one in the air, the other on the ground. Plastics can be inflammable, and chemistry sets can lead to explosions.

Never has more attention been paid to toys than in the modern world. There are enquiries into the needs of the child, the right methods of play, the correct approach to toys from every angle from the parents to the manufacturers. At the same time interest in toys of the past has reached a high level. There are Doll Clubs and Dollmakers' Circles galore, and toy collectors can scarcely satisfy their needs with the antique toys available. May good fortune attend the efforts of the collectors – since without their devotion and passionate study the toys which constitute so many of the illustrations of this book would certainly not have survived so long.

What is the eternal mystery of the toy, this 'pleasurable trifle' which exercises a fascination for children and adults alike? In my first chapter I defined the nature of the toy as being compounded of pleasure, imitation and fantasy. To these one should perhaps add an unchanging quality, which means that the same type of toy recurs again and again throughout history. A fashion in dress rises, declines and is then forgotten, but certain basic toys seem capable of holding the stage forever

288 A Dalek dressing-up suit modelled on the robots in the British TV science fiction serial, Dr Who. *Despite their sinister appearance and behaviour, children have taken the Daleks to their hearts. 289 An open side dolls' house designed by R. Limbrick*

290 The simple home-made go-cart remains a favourite toy, in spite of all the advances made in the toy industry, showing the infinite capacity of children for constructing and enjoying their own playthings

It is a pleasant if sobering thought that there have been practically no fundamental changes in toys since the days of the Egyptians, when almost all the types of our modern toys are discernible. There have, of course, been enormous advances in techniques of manufacture. There has also been a tremendous development in the attitude of the grown-up to the child, which one hopes has made childhood happier and more interesting. The fact remains that the archetypal toy is apparently so deeply rooted, like the play instinct of the child, that it cannot be eradicated by passing novelties. The fidelity of the child to its toy through the ages is one of the great love stories of history.

Recommended Further Reading

The following is a list of the principal authorities consulted in the writing of this book. To them and to their authors, the present writer wishes to acknowledge her debt with gratitude.

d'Allemagne, Henry. *Histoire des Jouets*, Paris, 1903

Bailey, C. S. *Toys and Whistles*, Viking, 1937

Baldet, Marcel. *Figurines et soldats de plomb*, Editions d'Art Gonthier, Paris

Becque de Fouquieres, L. *Les Jeux des Anciens*, Paris, 1869

Boehn, Max von. *Dolls and Puppets*, 1932

Born, Dr Wolfgang. 'Peepshows of the Renaissance', *Connoisseur*, February and April 1941

Chapuis, A and Droz, E. *Les Automates*, Neuchatel, 1949

Clark, John E. T. *Musical Boxes*, 1952

Cook, Olive. *Movement in Two Dimensions*, Hutchinson, 1963

Daiken, Leslie. *Children's Toys throughout the Ages*, Batsford, 1953

Daiken, Leslie. *World of Toys*, Lambarde Press, 1963

Early, Alice K. *English Dolls, Effigies and Puppets*, Batsford, 1955

Fawcett, Clara Hallard. *Dolls – A New Guide for Collectors*, 1964

Foley, Dan. *Toys Through the Ages*

Garratt, John G. *Model Soldiers: A Collector's Guide*, Seeley Service & Co

Gordon, Lesley. *Peepshow into Paradise: A History of Children's Toys*, Harrap, 1953

Greene, Vivien. *English Dolls' Houses*, Batsford, 1955

Gröber, Karl. *Children's Toys of Bygone Days*, Batsford, 1928

Gumuchian. *Les Livres de l'enfance du xv a xlx ieme siecle*

Hampe, Theodor. *Der Zinnsoldat, ein deutsches Spielzeug*

Harris, Henry. *Model Soldiers*, Weidenfeld & Nicolson, 1962

Haydon, A. *Spode and His Successors*, 1924

Hercik, Emmanuel. *Folk Toys*, 1951

Hertz, Louis H. *Handbook of Old American Toys*, Mark Haber, 1947

Hertz, Louis H. *Collecting Model Trains*, Simmons-Boardman, 1956

Hunt, Valerie V. *Recreation for the Handicapped*, Prentice-Hall, 1955

Isaacs, Susan. *Intellectual Growth in Young Children*, Routledge & Kegan Paul, 1930

Jacobs, Flora Gill. *A History of Dolls' Houses*, Cassell & Co, 1954

Jones, Barbara. *Unsophisticated Arts*

Klein, Anita E. *Child Life in Greek Art*, US, 1932

Lawrence, Evelyn Mary. *Friedrich Froebel and English Education*, University of London Press Ltd, 1952

Low, Frances H. *Queen Victoria's Dolls*, Newnes, 1894

Maingot, Eliane. *Les Automates*, Hachette, 1959

Marshall and McClintock, Inez. *Toys in America*, Public Affairs Press, Washington, 1961

Martin, Paul and Vaillant, Marcel. *Le monde merveilleux des soldats de plomb*, Paris

Metzger, Juliane. *Spielzeug damals, heute, andersno*, Ullstein Bücher

Muir, Percy. *English Children's Books*, Batsford, 1954

Oman, Charles. *English Silver Toys*, Apollo Magazine

Rabecq-Maillard, *M-M. Histoire du Jouet*, Hachette, 1962

Rees, Dr Elizabeth Lodge. *A Doctor Looks at Toys*, Charles C. Thomas, US, 1961

St George, Eleanor. *The Dolls of Yesterday*, Scribners, 1948

St George, Eleanor. *Dolls of Three Centuries*, Scribners, 1951

Simmons, H. R., (ed.) *Games & Toys: 50th Anniversary Issue*, June 1964

Speaight, George. *Juvenile Drama: The History of the English Toy Theatre*, 1946

Standing, Edwin Mortimer. *Maria Montessori: Her Life and Work*, Hollis & Co, 1957

Stevenson, R. L. *Penny Plain and Twopence Coloured*, 1884

Tippett, J. S. *Toys and Toy Makers*, Harpers, 1931

Wells, H. G. *Floor Games*, Dent & Sons, 1913

White, Gwen. *Dolls of the World*, Mills & Boon , 1962

Wilson, A. E. *Penny Plain, Twopence Coloured*

Author's Acknowledgments

In my researches I have received the help and advice of a wide variety of people, including toy manufacturers in many different countries, who have been extremely generous in supplying me with information. In particular I am especially indebted to the following for their assistance or encouragement: Mr Paul Abbatt and Miss Audrey Stephenson of Paul and Marjorie Abbatt Limited; Nancy, Lady Bagot; Mr Adrian Berry; Mrs E. Brooks; Rt Hon Edward Du Cann MP, then Minister of State, Board of Trade; Miss Faith Eaton; Mrs Marguerite Fawdry of Pollock's Toy Museum; Lord Glenconner; Dr Michael Grant; Mrs Graham Greene; Mr David Hicks; Miss Irene Blair Hickman; Frau Juliane Metzger; Professor Ivan Morris; Mr Percy Muir; Mr V. S. Naipaul; Mrs Mary Hillier; Signor Paolo Panzo of the Italian Embassy; Mr Anthony Powell; Mr Charles S. Raizen of Transogram Co Inc; Rt Hon Lord St Oswald; Mr Michael Raeburn of Weidenfeld and Nicolson; Mr I. H. Scott of Dean's Rag Book Co; Mr Edwin Smith; Mr W. Voorhees, President of *Playthings* USA; Mr Alfred Wells of the American Embassy; and lastly to my husband for his exemplary patience in reading the manuscript.

Acknowledgments

The publishers are grateful to the following for their help in assembling the illustrative material and for permission to reproduce photographs. *The names of photographers and photographic agencies are given in italics.*

CHAPTER 1

1 National Museum of Athens; 2 British Museum; 3, 4 Museum of Childhood, Edinburgh; 5 John Betjeman; 6 Museum of Childhood, Edinburgh; 7 London Museum; 8 Trustees of the Chatsworth Settlement; 9 London Museum; 10 Miss Blair Hickman, *A.C.Cooper*; 11 Musée d'Histoire de l'Education, Paris; 12 Tate Gallery, London; 13, 14 Miss Blair Hickman, *A.C.Cooper*; 15 Museum of Childhood, Edinburgh; 16 *Edwin Smith*; 17 By gracious permission of Her Majesty the Queen, *A.C.Cooper*; 18 Collection of F.S.Huber, *Edwin Smith*; 19 By courtesy of Hirschl & Adler Galleries, New York, *IBM Gallery, N.Y.*; 20 David Hicks, *Derrick Witty*; 21, 22 Lord Glenconner, *A.G.Ingram*

CHAPTER 2

23, 24 British Museum; 25, 26 Musée de Versailles; 27, 28, 29 British Museum; 30 University of California; 31 Museum of American Indian, New York; 32 British Museum; 33 Miss Blair Hickman, *A.C.Cooper*; 34 British Museum; 35 Staatliche Museen Ägyptische Abteilung, Berlin; 36 Museum of American Indian, New York; 37, 38, 39, 40, 41, 42, 43 British Museum; 44, 45 Collection of Miss Faith Eaton, *Illustrated LondonNews*; 46, 47 British Museum; 48, 49 Museum of Childhood, Edinburgh

CHAPTER 3

50, 51 British Museum; 52 Kunsthistorisches Museum, Vienna; 53 British Museum; 54 Louvre, *Hirmer Fotoarchiv Munich*; 55, 56, 57, 58 British Museum; 59 Gabinetto Fotografico Nazionale Rome; 60 British Museum; 61 National Museum of Athens; 62 Museo Nazionale Naples, *Alinari*

CHAPTER 4

63, 64 Strasbourg Historical Museum; 65 *Radio Times Hulton Picture Library*; 66, 67 Bodleian Library, Oxford; 68 Musée de Cluny, Paris, *Archives Photographiques*; 70 Strasbourg Historical Museum; 71 *Radio Times Hulton Picture Library*; 73, 74 British Museum; 75 Musée de l'Histoire de l'Education, *Josse-Lalance*; 76, 77, 78, 79 Bodleian Library, Oxford; 80 Kunsthistorisches Museum, Vienna; 81 Göttingen University Library

CHAPTER 5

82 Musée des Arts Decoratifs, Paris; 83 National Gallery, London, *A.C.Cooper*; 84 London Museum; 85 National Trust, *Edwin Smith*; 86 Germanisches Museum, Nuremberg; 87 Pinacoteca, Bologna; 88 Kunsthistorisches Museum, Vienna; 90 Nancy, Lady Bagot, Blithfield Hall; 91 British Museum; 92 *Radio Times Hulton Picture Library*; 93, 94, 95 Rijksmuseum, Amsterdam; 96 British Museum; 97 Courtesy of Mrs Imogene Anderson, New York, Smithsonian Institute; 98 British Museum; 99 Victoria and Albert Museum, *A.C.Cooper*; 100 Baron von Essen, *Kindlers Malerei Lexikon*; 101 By gracious permission of Her Majesty the Queen, *A.C.Cooper*; 102 British Museum

CHAPTER 6   103 Prado, Madrid, *Royal Academy*; 104 *Baron Studios*; 105 Mrs Graham Greene, *A.C.Cooper*; 106 *Country Life*; 107 Oberhaus Museum Passau; 108 Ditchley Park; 109, 110 Essex Institute Salem, Mass; 111 Metropolitan Museum of Art, New York, Sylmaris Collection; 112 Oberhaus Museum Passau; 113 The Dansk Folkemuseum, Copenhagen; 114 Munich Bavarian National Museum; 115 Musée d'Histoire de l'Education; 116, 117 Germanisches Museum, Nuremberg; 118 Städtische Kunstsammlungen, Augsburg; 119 Victoria and Albert Museum, London; 120 Musée d'Histoire de l'Education; 121 Walters Art Gallery, Baltimore, Maryland; 122 Courtesy of Maryland Historical Society, *IBM Gallery, New York*; 123 National Gallery of Canada; 124 *Blinkhorns, Oxford*; 125 Col M.E.St J.Barne

CHAPTER 7   126 Brooklyn Children's Museum; 127 Novosti Press Agency; 128 Warwick Toy Museum; 129 Percy Muir Collection, *Derrick Witty*; 130 Kunsthistorisches Museum; 131, 132, 133, 134 S.F.Sunley Ltd, *Derrick Witty*; 135 *Radio Times Hulton Picture Library*; 136 Collection of Joshua Logan, *Photo-Library Inc*; 137 American Museum in Britain, *William Morris*; 138 *Edwin Smith*; 139 S.F.Sunley Ltd, *Derrick Witty*; 140 Rottingdean Toy Museum, *Derrick Witty*; 141 Percy Muir Collection, *Derrick Witty*; 142 London Museum; 143 Walter Scott; 144 *A.C.Cooper*

CHAPTER 8   145 Percy Muir Collection, *Edwin Smith*; 146 *Bulloz*; 147, 148 Barnes Museum of Cinematography, *Edwin Smith*; 149 Pollock's Toy Museum; 150 British Museum; 151 Barnes Museum of Cinematography, *Edwin Smith*; 152 Pollock's Toy Museum; 153 British Museum; 154 Pollock's Toy Museum; 155, 156 Barnes Museum of Cinematography, *Edwin Smith*; 157 British Museum; 158 Victoria and Albert Museum, London; 159, 160, 161 Barnes Museum of Cinematography, *Edwin Smith*; 162 National Library of Ireland; 163 Barnes Museum of Cinematography, *Edwin Smith*; 164 Pollock's Toy Museum

CHAPTER 9   165 British Museum; 166 Tate Gallery; 167 New York Histrological Museum; 168 Musée de L'Armee, Paris; 169 British Museum; 170 Bethnal Green Museum, *A.C.Cooper*; 171 Angus McBean; 172, 173 John G.Garratt, *Edwin Smith*; 174 Bethnal Green Museum, *Edwin Smith*; 175 Miss Blair Hickman, *A.C.Cooper*; 176 London Museum; 177 The American Museum in Britain, *William Morris*; 178 Städtische Kunstsammlungen, Augsburg; 179, 180 New York Historical Society; 181 Norsk Folkemuseum, Oslo; 182 Museum of Childhood, Edinburgh; 183 The American Museum in Britain, *William Morris*; 184 Norsk Folkemuseum, Oslo; 185 By gracious permission of Her Majesty the Queen; 186 The American Museum in Britain, *William Morris*; 187 Rottingdean Toy Museum, *A.C.Cooper*; 189 *Radio Times Hulton Picture Library*

CHAPTER 10   190 By gracious permission of Her Majesty the Queen, *A.C.Cooper*; 191, 192 Miss Blair Hickman, *A.C.Cooper*; 193 Museum of the City of New York; 194, 195 Bethnal Green Museum, *A.C.Cooper*; 196 Lady Longford, *A.C.Cooper*; 197 Miss Blair Hickman, *A.C.Cooper*; 198 Nancy, Lady Bagot, Blithfield Hall, *Derrick Witty*; 199 Mrs Graham Greene, *A.C.Cooper*; 200 Pollock's Toy Museum; 201 Mrs Graham Greene, *Edwin Smith*; 202 Rijksmuseum; 203 Pollock's Toy Museum and John Noble; 204 Miss Blair Hickman, *A.C.Cooper*; 205, 206 Mrs Graham Greene, *A.C.Cooper*; 207 Miss Blair Hickman, *A.C.Cooper*; 208 Mrs Graham Greene, *A.C.Cooper*; 209 Bethnal Green Museum, *A.C.Cooper*; 210 Toy and Cupboard Museum

CHAPTER 11

211 Olive Jones, *Radio Times Hulton Picture Library*; 212 Illustrated London News; 214 Pollock's Toy Museum; 215 Rosemary Howard, Royal Academy of Arts; 216 Blackie and Sons; 217 Pollock's Toy Museum; 218 Bethnal Green Museum, *A.C.Cooper*; 220 *Anthony Panting*; 221 Mrs Graham Greene, *A.C.Cooper*; 222 Rottingdean Toy Museum, *Derrick Witty*; 223 Nancy, Lady Bagot, Blithfield Hall, *Derrick Witty*; 224 Dean's Rag Books; 225 Nancy, Lady Bagot, Blithfield Hall, *A.C.Cooper*; 226 Pollock's Toy Museum; 227 Musée d'Histoire de l'Education

CHAPTER 12

228 Bavarian Nationale Musée, *Claus Hansmann*; 229 Bethnal Green Museum, *A.C.Cooper*; 230 Germanisches National Museum; 231, 232 The New York Historical Society; 234 The American Museum in Britain, *William Morris*; 235 The American Museum in Britain; 236 Publishers Affairs Press, Washington, *Derrick Witty*; 237 The American Museum in Britain, *William Morris*; 238 Miss Blair Hickman, *A.C.Cooper*; 239 Bethnal Green Museum, *A.C.Cooper*; 240, 241 Miss Blair Hickman, *A.C.Cooper*; 242 Rottingdean Toy Museum, *Derrick Witty*; 243 Brooklyn Children's Museum; 244 Dean's Rag Book Co; 245 Galt, *Ken Garland*; 246 Dinky Toys Ltd; 247 Royal Botanic Gardens, Kew

CHAPTER 13

248 Dean's Rag Book Co; 249 *Radio Times Hulton Picture Library*; 250 Paul and Marjorie Abbatt (World Export) Ltd, *John Garner*; 251 Paul and Marjorie Abbatt (World Export) Ltd, *H.J.Orgler*; 252 By gracious permission of Her Majesty the Queen, *Harold White, FIBP, FRPS*; 253 Paul and Marjorie Abbatt; 254, 255 Paul and Marjorie Abbatt, *Colin Westwood*; 256 National Trust, Penburgh, *A.C.Cooper*; 257, 258 Dean's Rag Book Co; 259 Rottingdean Toy Museum, *Derrick Witty*

CHAPTER 14

260 Cheryl Playthings; 261 Cheryl Playthings, *Joseph Cordina*; 262 Lone Star Products, *Christopher Moore*; 263 Lone Star Products, *Transworld News Service*; 264, 265 *Edwin Smith*; 266 H.Jongejans; 267 Hassenfeld Brothers, USA; 268, 269 Revell, Inc; 270 Sunday Times; 271 *John Miles*; 272 *Master Art*; 273 James Galt, *Ken Garland*; 274 *Rayment Kirby*; 275 *Derrick Witty*; 276 Plastech Ltd; 277 Confederate Museum; 278 Observer; 279, 280 Rosebud Dolls Ltd; 281 C.Hanna-Barbera Productions Inc; 282 London Express; 283 By gracious permission of Her Majesty the Queen; 284 Triang Ltd; 285 *Edgar Brind Studios Ltd*; 286 Rottingdean Toy Museum, *Derrick Witty*; 287 International Model Aircraft Ltd; 288 Berwick Toy Company, *Batiste Publications*; 289 James Galt; 290 *Robert Mayne*

Index